Biotechnology Laboratory Manual: Techniques and Experiments

Dr. Sri Raghava

Dedication

This book is dedicated to all students, educators, and researchers who strive for excellence in the field of biotechnology.

To my mentors, whose guidance and wisdom have shaped my journey.

To my students, whose curiosity and passion inspire continuous learning and innovation.

To my family, for their unwavering support and encouragement.

May this manual serve as a valuable resource in your scientific endeavors, fostering discovery, knowledge, and progress.

Preface

This **Biotechnology Laboratory Manual: Techniques and Experiments** is designed to serve as a comprehensive guide for students, educators, and researchers in the field of biotechnology. The manual covers a wide range of essential laboratory techniques used in molecular biology, microbiology, biochemistry, and cell culture.

Each experiment in this manual is structured to provide a clear understanding of the underlying principles, step-by-step procedures, preparation of reagents, expected results, and discussion questions to reinforce the concepts. The manual is tailored to meet the curriculum requirements of university-level biotechnology courses and serves as a practical resource for conducting laboratory work efficiently and accurately.

Key Features:

- Step-by-step instructions for a wide range of biotechnology experiments.

- Preparation of reagents and materials to facilitate hands-on learning.

- Observations and results to aid in interpretation and understanding.

- Discussion questions to encourage critical thinking and deeper comprehension.

- Applicable to fields such as genetic engineering, microbiology, plant tissue culture, and biochemical analysis.

This manual aims to bridge the gap between theoretical knowledge and practical applications, ensuring students develop the necessary skills required for their academic and professional careers in biotechnology.

Dr. Sri Raghava

Laboratory DO's and DONT's

DO's:

1. Always wear appropriate personal protective equipment (PPE), including lab coats, gloves, and safety goggles.
2. Maintain a clean and organized workspace to avoid contamination and accidents.
3. Label all reagents, samples, and solutions properly to prevent mix-ups.
4. Follow standard operating procedures (SOPs) for each experiment.
5. Dispose of hazardous waste according to institutional guidelines.
6. Wash hands before and after laboratory work.
7. Report any accidents, spills, or breakages to the lab supervisor immediately.
8. Handle glassware with care to avoid breakage and injury.
9. Ensure proper calibration of instruments before use.
10. Work under aseptic conditions to avoid contamination.

DONT's:

1. Do not eat, drink, or store food in the laboratory.
2. Do not pipette by mouth; always use mechanical pipettes.

3. Do not leave equipment unattended while it is in operation.

4. Do not dispose of chemicals down the sink without proper neutralization.

5. Do not wear open-toed shoes or loose clothing in the lab.

6. Do not ignore safety signs and instructions.

7. Do not use damaged or cracked glassware.

8. Do not touch face, eyes, or mouth while handling chemicals.

9. Do not work alone in the lab without supervision.

10. Do not mix chemicals unless specified in the protocol.

Contents

Experiment 17: To study the effect of plasmolysis and deplasmolysis in onion peel.

Experiment 18: Hypo and Hypertonic Effects on Erythrocytes

Experiment 19: Study of Different Types of Cells in the Human Blood Smear/Differential Cell Counting of Blood

Experiment 20: Salivary Amylase Assay

Experiment 21: Mounting of Barr Bodies

Experiment 22: Study of Karyotyping in Onion and Humans (Normal and Abnormal)

Experiment 23: Mounting of Polytene Chromosomes

Experiment 24: DNA Isolation from Microorganisms

Experiment 25 : Isolation of DNA from Plant Source

Experiment 26: DNA Isolation from Animal Source

Experiment 27: DNA Estimation – Spectrophotometric Method

Experiment 28: Isolation of Plasmid DNA from bacterial cell

Experiment 29: Bacterial Transformation

Experiment 30:Gene Cloning

Experiment 31: Digestion of DNA using Restriction Enzymes and Analysis by Agarose Gel Electrophoresis

Experiment 32: Isolation of RNA from Cells

Experiment 33: Polymerase Chain Reaction (PCR)

Experiment 34: Determination of Blood Groups - Slide Agglutination Test

Experiment 35: Immuno-Precipitation

Experiment 36: Ouchterlony Double Diffusion

Experiment 37: Enzyme-Linked Immunosorbent Assay (ELISA)

Experiment 1: Qualitative Tests for Amin4o Acids

Aim: To identify the presence of different amino acids in a given sample through qualitative tests.

Principle: Amino acids contain characteristic functional groups that react with specific reagents to give distinct color changes, allowing their identification.

Preparation of Reagents:

1. **Ninhydrin Reagent:** Ninhydrin - 0.2 g, Acetone - 10 mL, Distilled water - up to 100 mL

2. **Xanthoproteic Reagent:** Concentrated nitric acid (HNO_3) - as required, Sodium hydroxide (NaOH) - 10% solution

3. **Millon's Reagent:** Mercuric nitrate - 1 g, Concentrated nitric acid - 10 mL, Distilled water - up to 100 mL

4. **Lead Acetate Reagent:** Lead acetate - 1 g, Distilled water - up to 100 mL

Test Name	Principle	Procedure	Observation
Ninhydrin Test	Ninhydrin reacts with free amino groups to produce a purple complex.	Add 1 mL of amino acid solution to a test tube, add a few drops of ninhydrin reagent, heat in a water bath for 5 minutes.	Purple or blue color indicates free amino groups.
Xanthoproteic Test	Aromatic amino acids react with nitric acid forming yellow nitro compounds.	Add 1 mL of amino acid solution to a test tube, add a few drops of conc. nitric acid, heat gently, cool, add NaOH.	Yellow color turns orange with NaOH (aromatic AAs).
Millon's Test	Tyrosine reacts with Millon's reagent to form a red precipitate.	Add 1 mL of amino acid solution to a test tube, add a few drops of Millon's reagent, heat gently.	Red precipitate indicates tyrosine.
Lead Acetate Test	Sulfur-containing amino acids form black precipitate with lead acetate.	Add 1 mL of amino acid solution to a test tube, add a few drops of lead acetate solution, heat gently.	Black precipitate indicates cysteine or methionine.

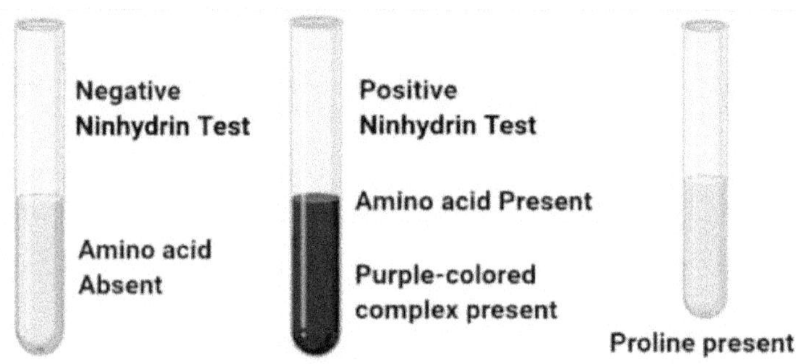

Ninhydrin test

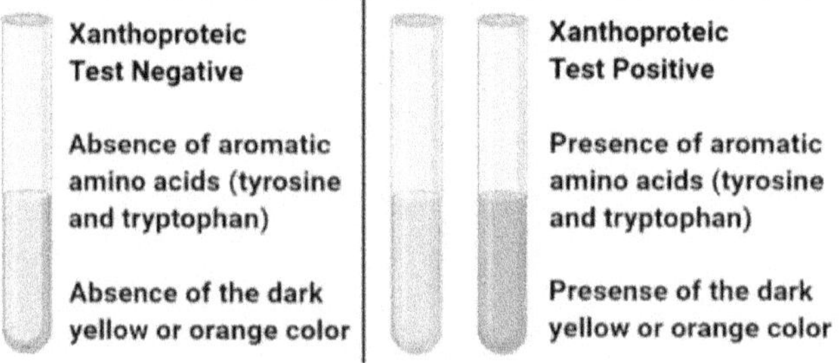

Xanthoproteic Test

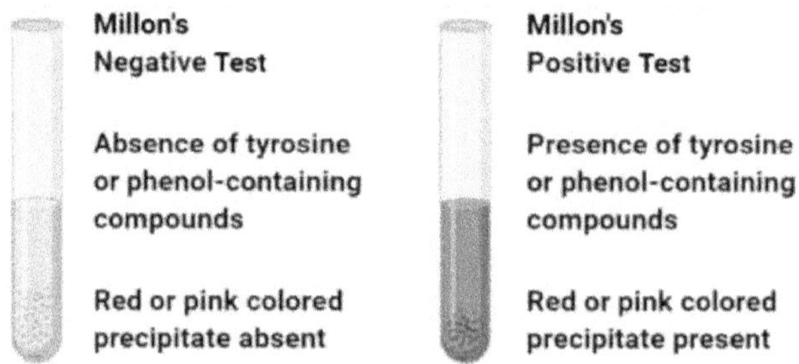

Millon's Test

Lead Acetate Test (Lead Sulfide test)

Experiment 2: Qualitative Tests for Carbohydrates

Aim: To identify the presence of carbohydrates in a given sample using qualitative tests.

Principle: Carbohydrates contain functional groups such as hydroxyl, aldehyde, or ketone groups, which can undergo specific reactions with various chemical reagents to produce characteristic color changes. These reactions help differentiate between reducing and non-reducing sugars, monosaccharides, disaccharides, and polysaccharides.

Preparation of Reagents

1. **Molisch's Reagent:**

   a) α-naphthol: 5 g
   b) Ethanol: 100 mL

2. **Benedict's Reagent:**

   a) Copper sulfate ($CuSO_4.5H_2O$): 17.3 g
   b) Sodium citrate: 173 g
   c) Sodium carbonate: 100 g
   d) Distilled water: up to 1 L

3. **Fehling's Solution:**

   a) Solution A: Copper sulfate (34.64 g) in 500 mL of distilled water
   b) Solution B: Potassium sodium tartrate (173 g) and sodium hydroxide (50 g) in 500 mL of distilled water

4. **Barfoed's Reagent:**

   a) Copper acetate: 4.5 g

b) Glacial acetic acid: 20 mL
c) Distilled water: up to 100 mL

5. **Iodine Solution:**

a) Iodine: 1 g
b) Potassium iodide: 2 g
c) Distilled water: up to 100 mL

Test Name	Principle	Procedure	Observation
Benedict's Test	Reducing sugars reduce Cu^{2+} to Cu^+, forming a colored precipitate.	Add 1 mL of carbohydrate solution to a test tube, add an equal volume of Benedict's reagent, heat in a water bath for 5 minutes.	Green, yellow, or brick-red precipitate.
Fehling's Test	Reducing sugars react with Fehling's reagent to form a red precipitate.	Add 1 mL of carbohydrate solution to a test tube, add equal volumes of Fehling's A and B solutions, heat gently.	Red precipitate confirms reducing sugars.
Iodine Test	Starch forms a blue-black complex with iodine.	Add 1 mL of carbohydrate solution to a test tube, add a few drops of iodine solution.	Blue-black color confirms starch.

Barfoed's Test	Monosaccharides reduce copper ions under acidic conditions.	Add 1 mL of carbohydrate solution to a test tube, add a few drops of Barfoed's reagent, heat in a water bath for 2 minutes.	Red precipitate confirms monosaccharides.
Molisch's Test	Carbohydrates react with sulfuric acid to form a violet-colored ring.	Add 1 mL of carbohydrate solution to a test tube, add a few drops of Molisch's reagent, add conc. sulfuric acid slowly along the sides.	Violet ring at the interface confirms carbohydrates.

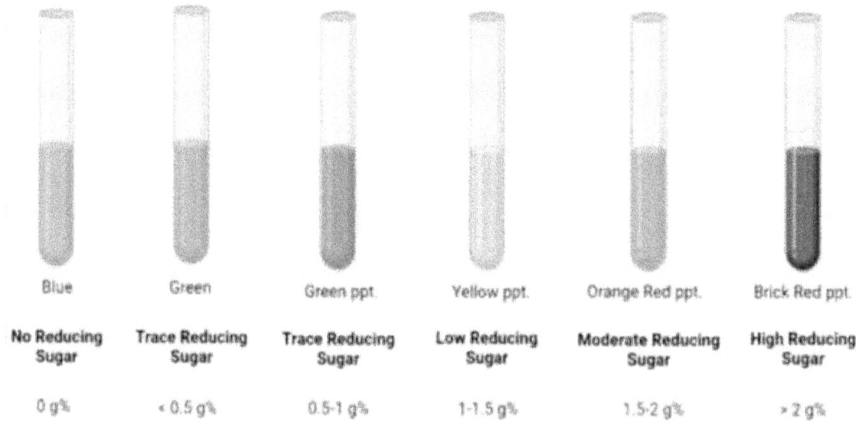

Benedicts test A) Negative B) Positive

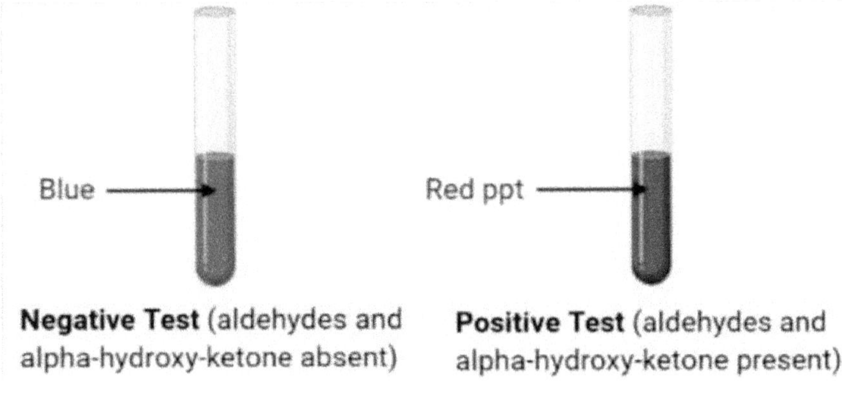

Fehling's Test

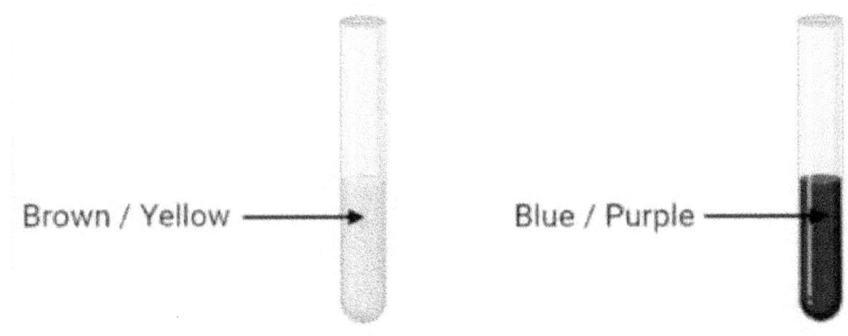

Iodine Test

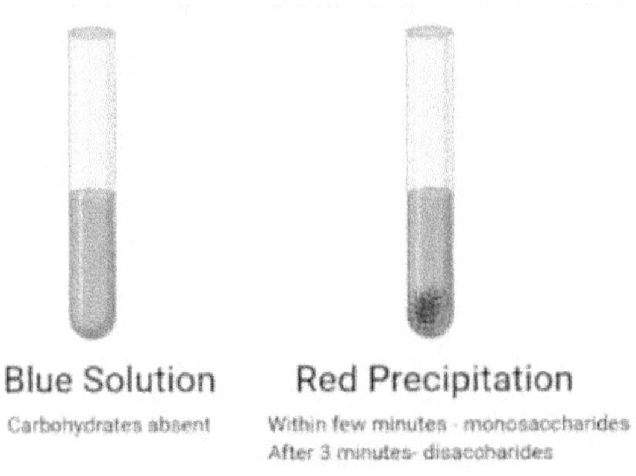

Barfoed's Test

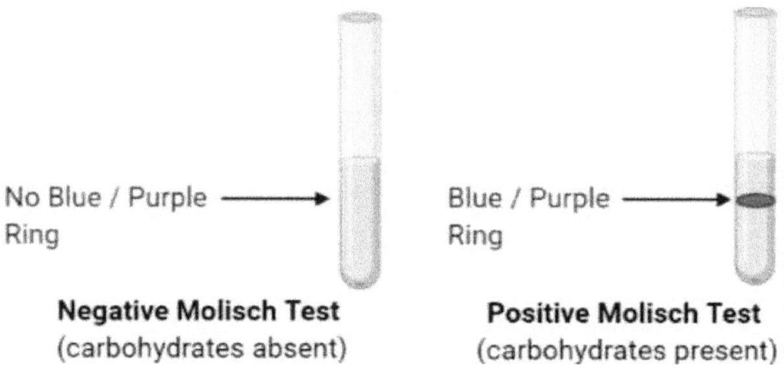

Molischs test

Precautions:

a) Handle concentrated acids with care.

b) Perform all heating steps using a water bath to avoid accidents.

c) Properly dispose of chemical waste as per lab guidelines.

Discussion Questions:

1. Why does ninhydrin produce a purple color with amino acids?

   ➤ Ninhydrin reacts with the free amino group of amino acids to form a colored complex known as Ruhemann's purple.

2. How can you differentiate between monosaccharides and disaccharides?

> Barfoed's test can be used to differentiate; monosaccharides give a positive result in a shorter time compared to disaccharides.

3. What is the principle behind Benedict's test?

> Benedict's reagent contains Cu^{2+} ions that get reduced to Cu^{+} in the presence of reducing sugars, forming a colored precipitate.

4. Why does iodine produce a blue-black color with starch?

> Iodine forms a complex with the helical structure of starch, resulting in a blue-black coloration.

5. What are the limitations of Fehling's test?

> Fehling's test cannot detect non-reducing sugars like sucrose without prior hydrolysis.

6. Why does lead acetate produce a black precipitate with sulfur-containing amino acids?

> Sulfur in amino acids reacts with lead acetate to form lead sulfide, which appears as a black precipitate.

7. How can proteins be distinguished from free amino acids in qualitative tests?

> Proteins may not give a positive ninhydrin test without hydrolysis, whereas free amino acids will react immediately.

Experiment 3: Estimation of Glucose by DNS Method

Aim: To estimate the concentration of glucose in a given sample using the DNS (3,5-dinitrosalicylic acid) method.

Principle: The DNS method is based on the reduction of 3,5-dinitrosalicylic acid by the aldehyde group of reducing sugars, leading to the formation of a reddish-brown complex. The intensity of the color developed is proportional to the glucose concentration and can be measured spectrophotometrically at 540 nm.

Preparation of Reagents:

1. **DNS Reagent**
    a) 1% 3,5-dinitrosalicylic acid (DNS) - 1 g
    b) 30% Sodium potassium tartrate - 30 g
    c) 0.4 M Sodium hydroxide (NaOH) - 8 g
    d) Distilled water - up to 1 L

2. **Glucose Standard Solution (1 mg/mL)**
    a) Dissolve 100 mg of glucose in 100 mL of distilled water.

3. **Rochelle Salt Solution**
    a) Sodium potassium tartrate - 40 g
    b) Distilled water - up to 100 mL

4. **Working Standard Solution**
    a) Dilute the stock glucose solution to obtain desired concentrations (0.2, 0.4, 0.6, 0.8, 1.0 mg/mL).

Procedure:

1. Prepare glucose standards of known concentrations (e.g., 0.2, 0.4, 0.6, 0.8, and 1.0 mg/mL).
2. Take 1 mL of the glucose solution (unknown sample or standard) in a test tube.
3. Add 3 mL of DNS reagent to each tube.
4. Heat the tubes in a boiling water bath for 5 minutes.
5. Allow the tubes to cool to room temperature.
6. Measure the absorbance of each sample at 540 nm using a spectrophotometer.
7. Plot a standard curve using the absorbance values of the glucose standards.
8. Determine the concentration of the unknown sample using the standard curve.

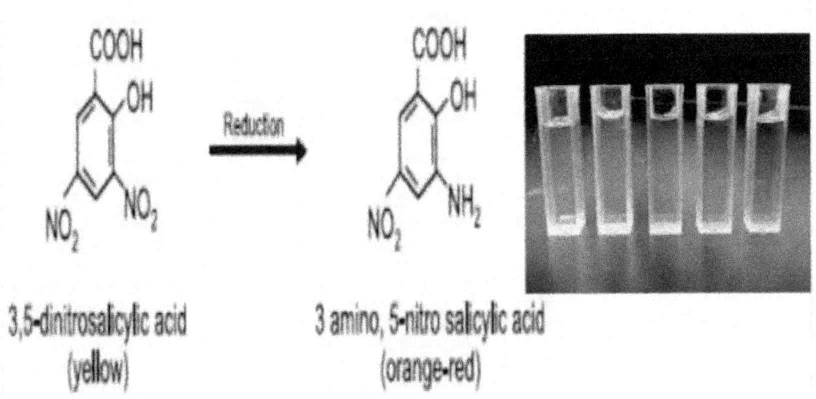

Results:

Record the absorbance values in the following table:

Glucose Concentration (mg/mL)	Absorbance at 540 nm
0.2	
0.4	
0.6	
0.8	
1.0	
Unknown Sample	

Graph:

Plot a graph of absorbance versus glucose concentration to determine the unknown sample concentration.

Precautions:

- Handle concentrated acids with care.
- Perform all heating steps using a water bath to avoid accidents.
- Properly dispose of chemical waste as per lab guidelines.

Discussion Questions:

1. What is the role of DNS reagent in glucose estimation?

➢ DNS reagent reacts with the reducing sugar to form a reddish-brown complex, which can be measured spectrophotometrically.

2. Why is heating necessary in the DNS method?

➢ Heating helps in the reduction of DNS by glucose and enhances color development.

3. Why do we use a standard curve in glucose estimation?

➢ A standard curve helps in determining the concentration of unknown samples by comparing absorbance values.

4. What could cause errors in glucose estimation using the DNS method?

➢ Errors can arise from improper calibration, contamination, or incorrect timing during heating.

5. How does the DNS method differ from other glucose estimation methods?

➢ The DNS method is simple and widely used but less sensitive compared to enzymatic methods like glucose oxidase-peroxidase assays.

Experiment 4: Estimation of Amino Acid by Ninhydrin Method

Aim: To estimate the concentration of amino acids in a given sample using the Ninhydrin method.

Principle: Ninhydrin reacts with free amino acids to form a colored complex known as Ruhemann's purple. The intensity of the color is proportional to the amino acid concentration and can be measured spectrophotometrically at 570 nm.

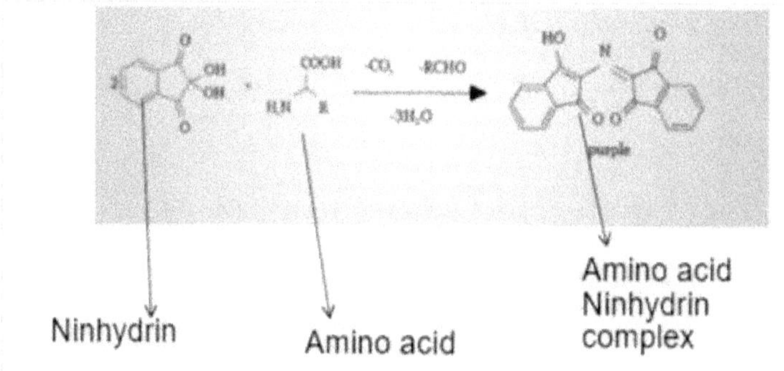

Procedure:

1. Prepare amino acid standards of known concentrations (e.g., 0.2, 0.4, 0.6, 0.8, and 1.0 mg/mL).
2. Take 1 mL of the amino acid solution (unknown sample or standard) in a test tube.
3. Add 2 mL of Ninhydrin reagent to each tube.
4. Heat the tubes in a boiling water bath for 10 minutes.
5. Allow the tubes to cool to room temperature.

6. Measure the absorbance of each sample at 570 nm using a spectrophotometer.

7. Plot a standard curve using the absorbance values of the amino acid standards.

8. Determine the concentration of the unknown sample using the standard curve.

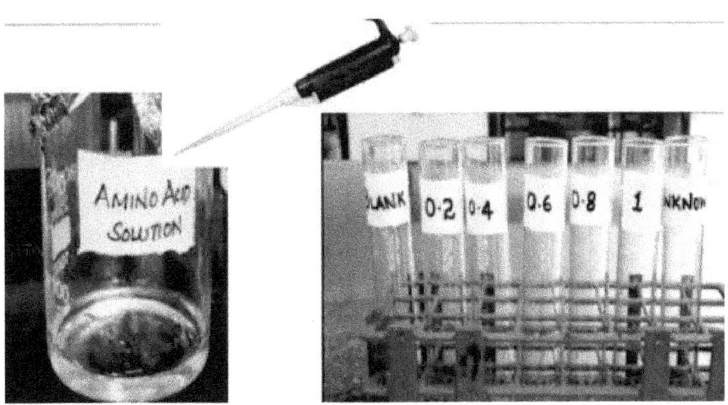

Results:

Record the absorbance values in the following table:

Amino Acid Concentration (mg/mL)	Absorbance at 570 nm
0.2	
0.4	
0.6	
0.8	
1.0	
Unknown Sample	

Graph:

Plot a graph of absorbance versus amino acid concentration to determine the unknown sample concentration.

Discussion Questions:

1. What is the principle of the Ninhydrin test?
   - ➢ Ninhydrin reacts with free amino groups to produce Ruhemann's purple, which is measured at 570 nm.
2. Why is it necessary to heat the reaction mixture?
   - ➢ Heating accelerates the reaction and ensures complete development of the color complex.
3. How can the concentration of an unknown amino acid sample be determined?
   - ➢ By plotting a standard curve and comparing the absorbance of the unknown sample.
4. What precautions should be taken while performing the experiment?
   - ➢ Use fresh reagents, avoid contamination, and measure absorbance promptly after cooling.
5. Why does Ninhydrin react with proline differently than other amino acids?
   - ➢ Proline is a secondary amine and forms a yellow complex instead of the usual purple.

Experiment 5: Separation of Amino Acids by Paper Chromatography

Aim: To separate and identify different amino acids in a mixture using paper chromatography.

Principle: Paper chromatography is based on the differential partitioning of amino acids between the stationary phase (paper) and the mobile phase (solvent). Amino acids migrate at different rates depending on their solubility and interaction with the stationary phase, allowing for their separation.

Procedure:

1. Take a Whatman filter paper strip and draw a pencil line 2 cm from the bottom.
2. Spot the amino acid mixture onto the pencil line using a capillary tube.
3. Allow the spot to dry completely.
4. Prepare the chromatography chamber by adding the solvent mixture (e.g., butanol:acetic acid:water in 4:1:1 ratio).
5. Place the paper strip in the chamber with the sample spot above the solvent level.
6. Close the chamber and allow the solvent to travel up the paper by capillary action.
7. Once the solvent front reaches near the top, remove the paper and allow it to dry.

8. Spray the dried paper with ninhydrin reagent and heat at 100°C to develop spots.

Results:

Calculate the retention factor (Rf) for each amino acid using the formula:

$$Rf = \frac{\textbf{Distance from origin run by the compound}}{\textbf{Distance from origin run by the solvent}}$$

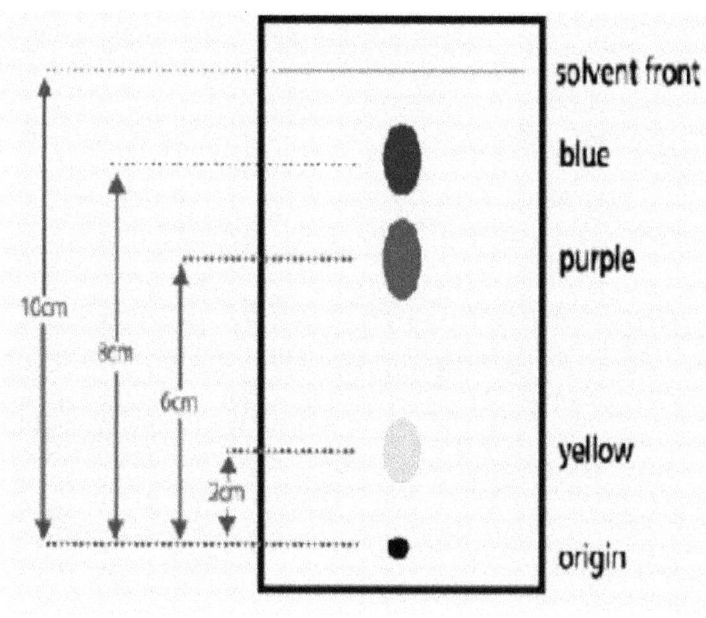

Record observations in the following table:

Amino Acid	Distance traveled by Amino Acid (cm)	Distance traveled by Solvent Front (cm)	Rf Value

Discussion Questions:

1. What factors affect the separation of amino acids in paper chromatography?

    ➢ Solvent polarity, paper type, and interactions with the stationary phase.

2. Why is ninhydrin used in this experiment?

    ➢ Ninhydrin reacts with amino acids to produce a colored product, making them visible.

3. How do you calculate the Rf value?

    ➢ By dividing the distance traveled by the amino acid by the distance traveled by the solvent front.

4. Why is it important to allow the sample to dry before running the chromatography?

    ➢ To prevent smudging and ensure accurate results.

5. What are the applications of paper chromatography in biotechnology?

    ➢ It is used for amino acid profiling, drug testing, and food quality analysis.

Experiment 6: Separation of Lipids by Thin Layer Chromatography (TLC)

Aim: To separate and identify different lipid components in a mixture using thin-layer chromatography (TLC).

Principle: TLC is a technique based on the differential migration of lipids over a stationary phase (silica gel) using a mobile phase (solvent system). Lipids are separated based on their polarity, and visualization is achieved by using specific staining reagents.

Preparation of Reagents:

1. **Mobile Phase (Solvent System)**
   a) Hexane: Diethyl ether: Acetic acid (80:20:1 v/v/v)

2. **Developing Chamber**
   a) Saturate with the mobile phase for at least 30 minutes before running the TLC.

3. **Silica Gel TLC Plates**
   a) Pre-coated silica gel plates (20 cm × 20 cm)

4. **Lipid Sample Preparation**
   a) Dissolve lipid extract in chloroform at a concentration of 10 mg/mL.

5. **Detection Reagents**
   a) Iodine vapor for visualization
   b) Phosphomolybdic acid solution (5% in ethanol) for staining

Procedure:

1. Prepare a TLC plate by coating it with a thin layer of silica gel and allowing it to dry.
2. Draw a pencil line 1 cm above the bottom of the plate.
3. Apply the lipid sample mixture on the pencil line using a micropipette.
4. Place the TLC plate in a developing chamber containing the solvent system (e.g., hexane:diethyl ether:acetic acid in 80:20:1 ratio).
5. Allow the solvent to ascend the plate by capillary action until it reaches near the top.
6. Remove the plate and allow it to air dry.
7. Spray the plate with iodine vapor or phosphomolybdic acid for visualization of separated lipid spots.

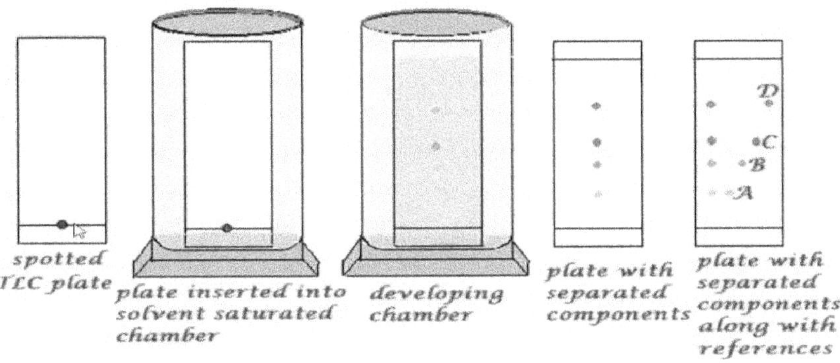

Results:

Calculate the retention factor (Rf) for each lipid component using the formula:

Record observations in the following table:

Lipid Component	Distance traveled by Lipid (cm)	Distance traveled by Solvent Front (cm)	Rf Value

Discussion Questions:

1. What is the principle behind TLC separation of lipids?
   - ➢ Separation is based on differential migration of lipid molecules on the stationary phase.
2. Why is silica gel used as the stationary phase in TLC?
   - ➢ Silica gel provides good separation due to its high polarity and adsorption properties.
3. What is the role of the solvent system in lipid separation?
   - ➢ The solvent system determines the migration and separation of lipid components based on polarity.
4. How can lipid spots be visualized after separation?
   - ➢ By using specific staining reagents such as iodine vapor or phosphomolybdic acid.
5. What are the applications of TLC in lipid analysis?
   - ➢ It is used for lipid profiling, quality control, and detecting lipid composition in biological samples.

Experiment 7: Estimation of DNA by Diphenylamine (DPA) Method

Aim: To estimate the concentration of DNA in a given sample using the Diphenylamine (DPA) method.

Principle: The DPA method is based on the reaction of deoxyribose sugar in DNA with diphenylamine under acidic conditions to form a blue-colored complex. The intensity of the color developed is proportional to the DNA concentration and can be measured spectrophotometrically at 595 nm.

Preparation of Reagents:

1. **DPA Reagent**
   a) Diphenylamine - 1.5 g
   b) Glacial acetic acid - 100 mL
   c) Concentrated sulfuric acid - 2.5 mL
   d) Distilled water - up to 1 L

2. **Standard DNA Solution (100 µg/mL)**
   a) Dissolve 10 mg of DNA in 100 mL of distilled water.

3. **Perchloric Acid Solution (2N)**
   a) Perchloric acid - 17.1 mL
   b) Distilled water - up to 100 mL

4. **Working Standard Solution**
   a) Dilute the stock DNA solution to obtain desired concentrations (20, 40, 60, 80, 100 µg/mL).

Procedure:

1. Prepare DNA standards of known concentrations (e.g., 20, 40, 60, 80, 100 µg/mL).
2. Take 1 mL of the DNA solution (unknown sample or standard) in a test tube.
3. Add 2 mL of DPA reagent to each tube.
4. Heat the tubes in a boiling water bath for 10 minutes.
5. Allow the tubes to cool to room temperature.
6. Measure the absorbance of each sample at 595 nm using a spectrophotometer.

7. Plot a standard curve using the absorbance values of the DNA standards.

8. Determine the concentration of the unknown sample using the standard curve.

Results:

Record the absorbance values in the following table:

DNA Concentration (µg/mL)	Absorbance at 595 nm
20	
40	
60	
80	
100	
Unknown Sample	

Graph:

Plot a graph of absorbance versus DNA concentration to determine the unknown sample concentration.

Discussion Questions:

1. What is the principle behind the DPA method for DNA estimation?

> ➢ The method relies on the reaction between deoxyribose sugar in DNA and diphenylamine under acidic conditions to produce a blue-colored complex.

2. Why is heating required in the DPA method?

> ➢ Heating accelerates the reaction and ensures complete color development.

3. How does the DPA method differentiate between DNA and RNA?

> ➢ The method is specific for DNA as RNA does not contain deoxyribose sugar.

4. What precautions should be taken while performing the experiment?

> ➢ Proper handling of reagents, accurate pipetting, and avoiding contamination.

5. What are the applications of the DPA method in molecular biology?

> ➢ It is used in quantifying DNA in biological samples and forensic investigations.

Experiment 8: Estimation of RNA by Orcinol Method

Aim:b To estimate the concentration of RNA in a given sample using the Orcinol method.

Principle: The Orcinol method is based on the reaction of ribose sugar in RNA with orcinol in the presence of ferric chloride under acidic conditions, producing a green-colored complex. The intensity of the color is proportional to the RNA concentration and can be measured spectrophotometrically at 660 nm.

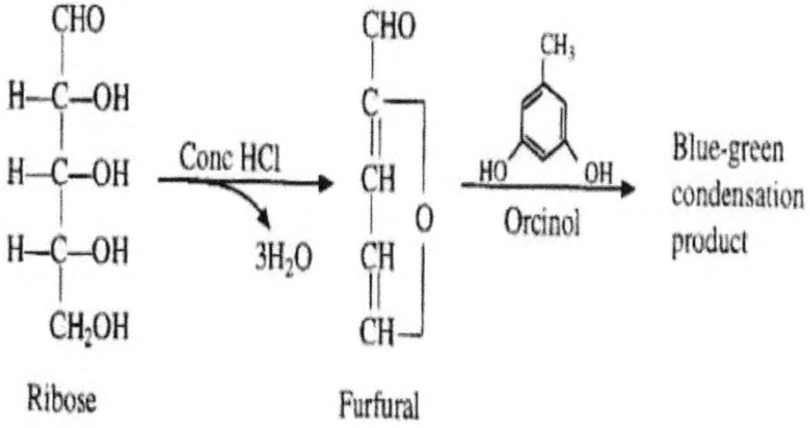

Preparation of Reagents:

1. **Orcinol Reagent:**
    a) Orcinol - 0.5 g
    b) Ferric chloride (0.1% w/v) - 0.25 mL
    c) Concentrated hydrochloric acid - 50 mL
    d) Distilled water - up to 1 L
2. **Standard RNA Solution (100 µg/mL):**
    a) Dissolve 10 mg of RNA in 100 mL of distilled water.

3. **Working Standard Solution:**

   a) Dilute the stock RNA solution to obtain desired concentrations (20, 40, 60, 80, 100 µg/mL).

Procedure:

1. Prepare RNA standards of known concentrations (e.g., 20, 40, 60, 80, 100 µg/mL).
2. Take 1 mL of the RNA solution (unknown sample or standard) in a test tube.
3. Add 2 mL of Orcinol reagent to each tube.
4. Heat the tubes in a boiling water bath for 20 minutes.
5. Allow the tubes to cool to room temperature.
6. Measure the absorbance of each sample at 660 nm using a spectrophotometer.
7. Plot a standard curve using the absorbance values of the RNA standards.
8. Determine the concentration of the unknown sample using the standard curve.

Results:

Record the absorbance values in the following table:

Vol. of Std. RNA	Vol. of Distilled water	RNA Concentration (µg/mL)	Absorbance at 660 nm
		20	
		40	
		60	
		80	
		100	
		Unknown Sample	

Graph:

Plot a graph of absorbance versus RNA concentration to determine the unknown sample concentration.

Discussion Questions:

1. What is the principle behind the Orcinol method for RNA estimation?

   ➢ The method relies on the reaction between ribose sugar in RNA and orcinol under acidic conditions to produce a green-colored complex.

2. Why is heating required in the Orcinol method?

   ➢ Heating accelerates the reaction and ensures complete color development.

3. How does the Orcinol method differentiate between RNA and DNA?

    ➢ The method is specific for RNA as it detects ribose sugar, which is absent in DNA.

4. What precautions should be taken while performing the experiment?

    ➢ Proper handling of reagents, accurate pipetting, and avoiding contamination.

5. What are the applications of the Orcinol method in molecular biology?

    ➢ It is used in quantifying RNA in biological samples and forensic investigations.

Experiment 9: Determination of pI of Amino Acid by Titration Method

Aim: To determine the isoelectric point (pI) of an amino acid by titration method.

Principle: The isoelectric point (pI) is the pH at which an amino acid carries no net electrical charge. It is determined by titrating the amino acid solution with a strong acid or base and monitoring pH changes. The pI is the pH value at which the amino acid has equal positive and negative charges.

Preparation of Reagents:

1. **Amino Acid Solution (0.1 M):**
   a) Dissolve the required amount of amino acid in distilled water to prepare a 0.1 M solution.

2. **Hydrochloric Acid (HCl) Solution (0.1 M):**
   a) Dilute concentrated HCl with distilled water to obtain a 0.1 M solution.

3. **Sodium Hydroxide (NaOH) Solution (0.1 M):**
   a) Dissolve the appropriate amount of NaOH pellets in distilled water to prepare a 0.1 M solution.

4. **pH Indicator (Phenolphthalein or pH Meter Calibration Buffers):**
   a) Prepare standard buffer solutions of pH 4.0, 7.0, and 10.0 for calibration.

Procedure:

1. Prepare a 0.1 M solution of the amino acid in distilled water.
2. Calibrate the pH meter using standard buffer solutions.
3. Take 50 mL of the amino acid solution in a beaker and place the pH electrode in it.
4. Titrate the solution with 0.1 M NaOH (for acidic amino acids) or 0.1 M HCl (for basic amino acids) while stirring continuously.
5. Record the pH after each addition of titrant.
6. Plot a titration curve with pH on the y-axis and volume of titrant on the x-axis.
7. Determine the pI by identifying the midpoint of the steepest section of the curve.

Results:

Record the titration data in the following table:

Volume of Titrant (mL)	pH

Graph:

Plot a graph of pH versus volume of titrant to determine the pI.

Discussion Questions:

1. What is the significance of determining the pI of an amino acid?
   - The pI is important for understanding solubility and charge properties of amino acids in biological systems.
2. Why is pH monitoring crucial during titration?
   - Monitoring pH helps identify the point at which the amino acid is electrically neutral.
3. How does the titration curve help in determining pI?
   - The curve shows inflection points, and the pI is at the midpoint of the buffering region.
4. What factors can affect the accuracy of pI determination?
   - Factors include temperature, ionic strength, and purity of the amino acid sample

Experiment 10: Determination of Iodine Number and Acetyl Number of a Lipid

Aim: To determine the iodine number and acetyl number of a lipid sample.

Iodine Number

Principle: The iodine number measures the degree of unsaturation in a lipid. It is determined by the amount of iodine absorbed by the double bonds present in the fatty acids of the lipid.

Preparation of Reagents:

1. **Iodine Number Reagent:**
    a) Wijs solution (Iodine monochloride in glacial acetic acid) - 25 mL
    b) Potassium iodide (KI) solution (10%) - 10 mL
    c) Sodium thiosulfate (0.1 N) - as required
    d) Starch indicator solution (1%) - 2 mL

2. **Acetyl Number Reagent:**
    a) Acetic anhydride - 20 mL
    b) Pyridine - 10 mL
    c) Sodium hydroxide (0.1 N) - as required
    d) Phenolphthalein indicator - 2 drops

Procedure:

1. Weigh accurately 0.5 g of the lipid sample and dissolve in chloroform.
2. Add 25 mL of Wijs solution and allow the reaction to proceed in the dark for 30 minutes.
3. Add potassium iodide solution and titrate with sodium thiosulfate using starch as an indicator.
4. Perform a blank titration and calculate the iodine number using the formula:

Iodine Number Formula:

$$\text{Iodine Number} = (B-S) \times N \times 12.69 / W$$

Where:

B = Volume of sodium thiosulfate used for blank (mL)

S = Volume of sodium thiosulfate used for sample (mL)

N = Normality of sodium thiosulfate

W = Weight of lipid sample (g)

Acetyl Number

Principle: The acetyl number indicates the hydroxyl group content in a lipid by determining the amount of acetic acid liberated by saponification.

Procedure:

1. Weigh accurately 1 g of the lipid sample and dissolve in pyridine.
2. Add acetic anhydride and reflux for 1 hour.
3. Cool and titrate the liberated acetic acid with sodium hydroxide using phenolphthalein as an indicator.
4. Perform a blank titration and calculate the acetyl number using the formula:

Acetyl Number Formula:

$$\text{Acetyl Number} = (S-B) \times N \times 60.05/w$$

Where, S = Volume of NaOH used for the sample (mL)

B = Volume of NaOH used for blank (mL)

N = Normality of NaOH

W = Weight of lipid sample (g)

Discussion Questions and Answers:

1. **Why is the iodine number important in lipid analysis?**
   - ➢ The iodine number indicates the degree of unsaturation in lipids, affecting stability, shelf life, and nutritional value.

2. **What is the significance of the acetyl number in lipid characterization?**

> ➢ The acetyl number provides information about hydroxyl content in lipids, influencing emulsification and functionality.

3. **How does the degree of unsaturation affect the iodine number?**

> ➢ A higher degree of unsaturation results in a higher iodine number, as more double bonds react with iodine.

4. **What are the practical applications of determining the iodine and acetyl numbers in food industries?**

> ➢ These values aid in quality control, formulation of lipid-based products, and ensuring consistency in edible oils and fats.

Experiment 11: Agarose Gel Electrophoresis of DNA

Aim: To separate and analyze DNA fragments using agarose gel electrophoresis.

Principle: Agarose gel electrophoresis is a technique used to separate DNA fragments based on their size. DNA molecules migrate through the agarose gel matrix under the influence of an electric field, with smaller fragments moving faster than larger ones.

Preparation of Reagents for Agarose Gel Electrophoresis

1. **TAE Buffer (50X stock solution)**
   a) Tris base - 242 g
   b) Acetic acid - 57.1 mL
   c) EDTA (0.5 M, pH 8.0) - 100 mL
   d) Distilled water - up to 1 L

2. **Agarose Gel (1%)**
   a) Agarose - 1 g
   b) TAE buffer (1X) - 100 mL
   c) Heat the mixture until fully dissolved.

3. **Ethidium Bromide Staining Solution**
   a) Ethidium bromide - 10 mg
   b) Distilled water - 1 L

4. **Loading Dye (6X Solution)**
   a) Bromophenol blue - 0.25% (w/v)
   b) Xylene cyanol FF - 0.25% (w/v)
   c) Glycerol - 30% (v/v)
   d) Distilled water - up to 10 mL

5. DNA Ladder (Marker Preparation)

a) Purchase commercially available DNA ladder for size estimation.

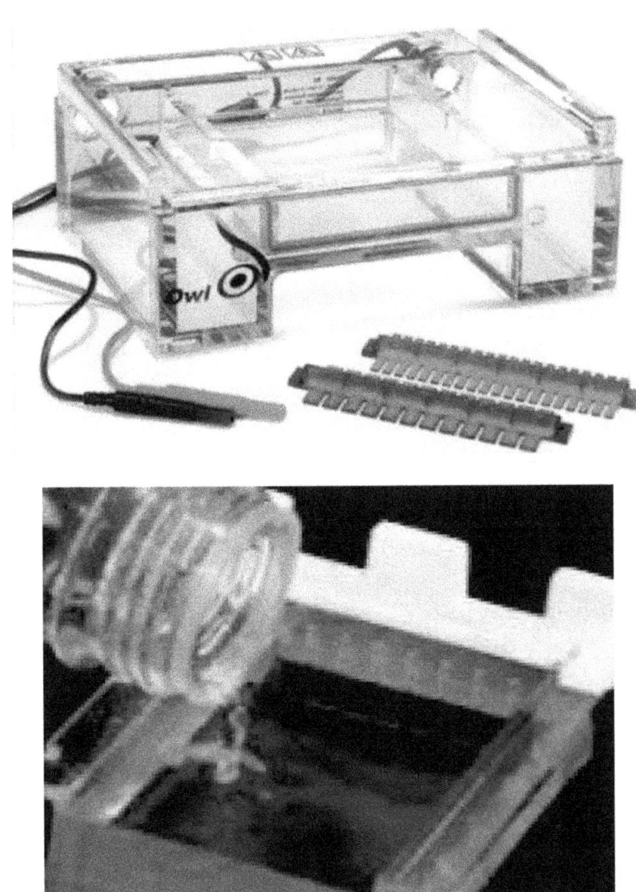

Agarose gel electrophoresis unit and Casting of Gel

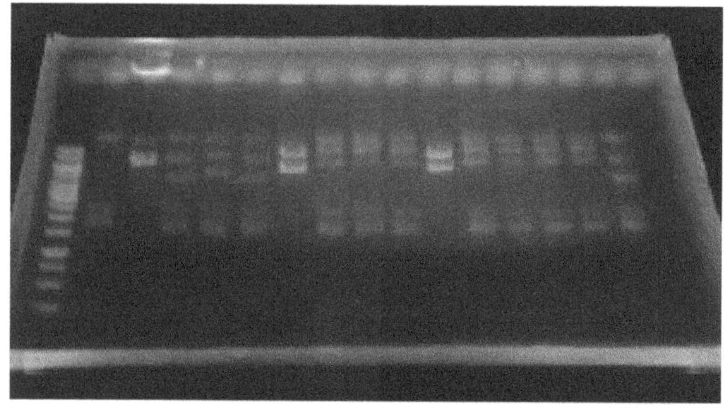

Observation of gel under UV illuminator

Procedure:

1. Prepare a 1% agarose gel by dissolving agarose in TAE buffer and heating until fully dissolved.
2. Pour the molten gel into a casting tray with a comb to form wells and allow it to solidify.
3. Load the DNA samples and molecular weight markers into the wells.
4. Run the gel at 100V for 30-45 minutes.
5. Stain the gel with ethidium bromide or SYBR Green.
6. Visualize the DNA bands under UV light.

Results:

Compare the migration of DNA samples with the molecular weight marker to determine fragment sizes.

Discussion Questions and Answers:

1. **What factors affect DNA migration in agarose gel electrophoresis?**

    ➤ Factors include gel concentration, voltage applied, and DNA fragment size.

2. **Why is ethidium bromide used in DNA electrophoresis?**

    ➤ It intercalates between DNA bases and fluoresces under UV light, allowing visualization of DNA bands.

3. **What is the purpose of the loading dye in DNA electrophoresis?**

    ➤ It provides color for sample tracking and increases the density of the sample, ensuring it sinks into the well.

4. **How does agarose gel concentration affect DNA separation?**

    ➤ Higher concentrations resolve smaller DNA fragments better, while lower concentrations separate larger fragments effectively.

Experiment 12: Protein Precipitation and Separation by SDS-PAGE

Aim: To precipitate and separate proteins using Sodium Dodecyl Sulfate Polyacrylamide Gel Electrophoresis (SDS-PAGE).

Principle:

SDS-PAGE is an electrophoretic technique used to separate proteins based on their molecular weight. Proteins are denatured using SDS, which imparts a uniform negative charge, allowing separation solely based on size.

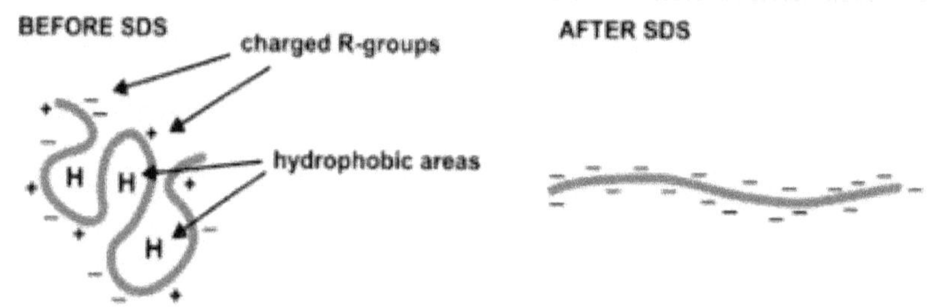

Preparation of Reagents for SDS-PAGE

1. **Resolving Gel Solution (12%)**
   a) Acrylamide/Bis solution (30%) - 4.0 mL
   b) 1.5 M Tris-HCl (pH 8.8) - 2.5 mL
   c) 10% SDS - 100 µL
   d) 10% Ammonium persulfate (APS) - 50 µL
   e) TEMED - 5 µL
   f) Distilled water - up to 10 mL
2. **Stacking Gel Solution (5%)**

a) Acrylamide/Bis solution (30%) - 0.67 mL

b) 0.5 M Tris-HCl (pH 6.8) - 1.25 mL

c) 10% SDS - 50 μL

d) 10% Ammonium persulfate (APS) - 25 μL

e) TEMED - 5 μL

f) Distilled water - up to 5 mL

3. **Running Buffer (1X Tris-Glycine-SDS Buffer)**

a) Tris base - 3.0 g

b) Glycine - 14.4 g

c) SDS - 1 g

d) Distilled water - up to 1 L

4. **Sample Loading Buffer (2X Laemmli Buffer)**

a) Tris-HCl (pH 6.8) - 125 mM

b) SDS - 4%

c) Glycerol - 20%

d) β-mercaptoethanol - 10%

e) Bromophenol blue - 0.01%

5. **Staining Solution (Coomassie Brilliant Blue)**

a) Coomassie Brilliant Blue R-250 - 0.25 g

b) Methanol - 50 mL

c) Acetic acid - 10 mL

d) Distilled water - up to 100 mL

6. **Destaining Solution**

a) Methanol - 50 mL

b) Acetic acid - 10 mL

c) Distilled water - up to 100 mL

Procedure:

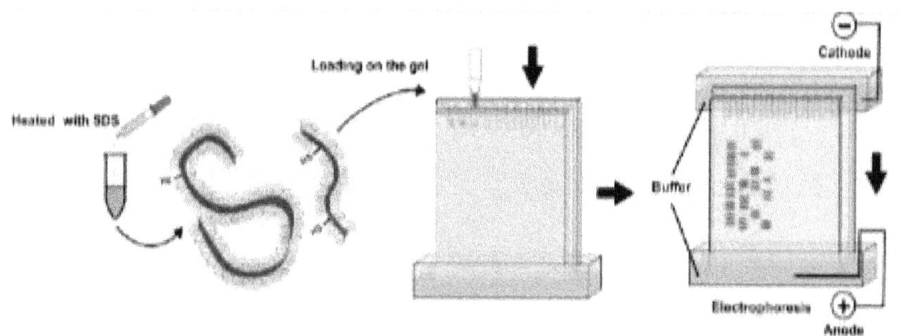

Protein Precipitation:

1. Take 10 mL of protein sample in a centrifuge tube.

2. Add an equal volume of 10% trichloroacetic acid (TCA).

3. Incubate on ice for 30 minutes.

4. Centrifuge at 10,000 rpm for 10 minutes.

5. Discard the supernatant and wash the pellet with cold acetone.

6. Dry the precipitated protein pellet and dissolve it in SDS loading buffer.

SDS-PAGE:

1. Prepare the polyacrylamide gel (separating and stacking gel) with appropriate concentrations.
2. Load the protein samples and molecular weight markers into the wells.
3. Run the gel at 100V until the dye front reaches the bottom.
4. Stain the gel using Coomassie Brilliant Blue and destain to visualize the protein bands.

Results:

Analyze the separated protein bands by comparing them with the molecular weight marker.

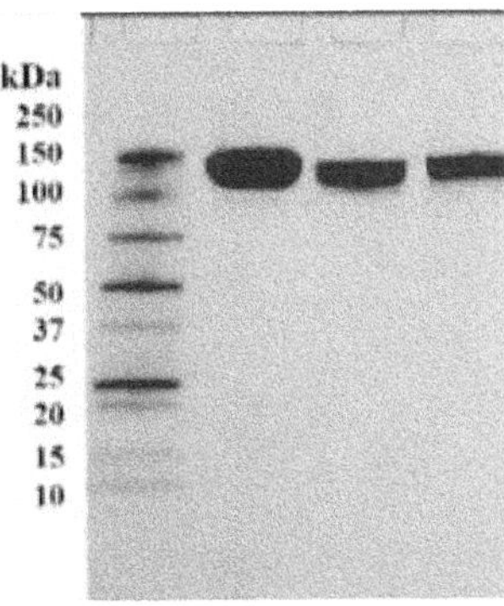

Discussion Questions and Answers:

1. **Why is SDS used in protein electrophoresis?**

> ➢ SDS denatures proteins and provides a uniform negative charge, allowing separation based on size only.

2. **What is the role of stacking and separating gels in SDS-PAGE?**

> ➢ The stacking gel concentrates proteins into a narrow band, while the separating gel resolves them based on molecular weight.

3. **Why is protein precipitation done before electrophoresis?**

> ➢ It concentrates the proteins and removes contaminants that may interfere with separation.

4. **What factors can affect protein separation in SDS-PAGE?**

> ➢ Gel concentration, sample preparation, and electrophoresis conditions.

Experiment 13: Preparation of Slides of Mitosis from Onion Root Tip Cells

Aim: To prepare and observe mitotic stages in onion root tip cells under a microscope.

Principle: Onion root tips contain actively dividing cells, making them ideal for studying mitosis. Hydrochloric acid softens the tissue, and acetocarmine or orcein stains the chromosomes, allowing observation of different mitotic phases.

Preparation of Reagents:

1. **Hydrochloric Acid Solution (1N):**
    a) Concentrated HCl - 8.3 mL
    b) Distilled water - up to 100 mL

2. **Acetocarmine Stain:**
    a) Acetocarmine - 1 g
    b) 45% Acetic acid - 100 mL

Procedure:

1. Take fresh onion roots and cut the root tips (1-2 cm).
2. Boil the root tips in 1N HCl for 5 minutes.
3. Wash the root tips with distilled water.
4. Stain the root tips with acetocarmine for 10-15 minutes.
5. Place the stained root tip on a slide, add a drop of water, and cover with a coverslip.
6. Gently press the coverslip to squash the cells and observe under a microscope.

Result:

Various stages of mitosis such as prophase, metaphase, anaphase, and telophase can be observed.

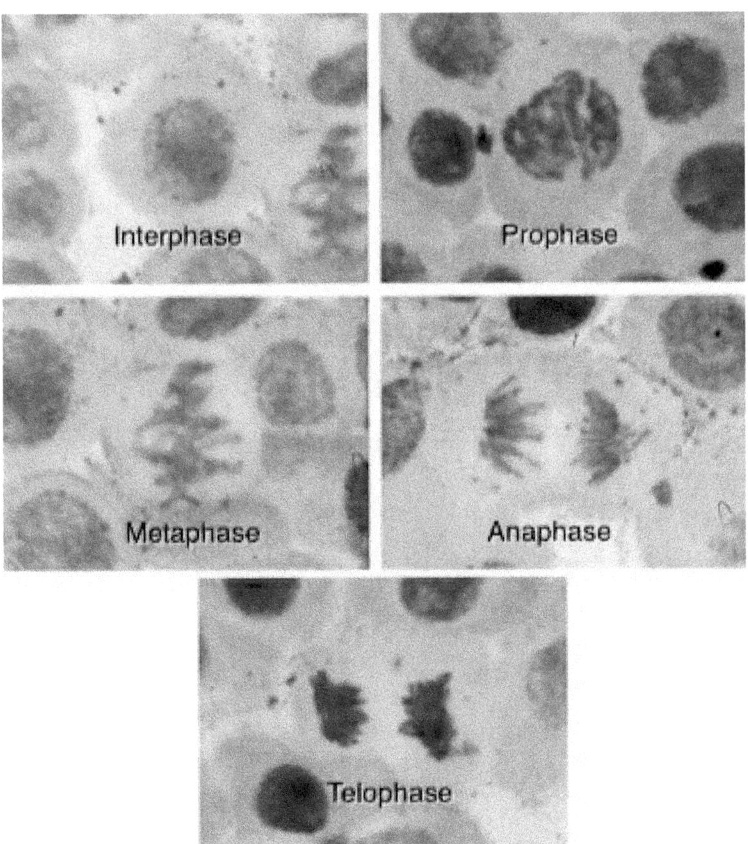

Discussion Questions and Answers:

1. **Why is the onion root tip used for mitosis study?**

   ➢ It contains actively dividing cells with clearly visible chromosomes.

2. **What is the role of hydrochloric acid in the experiment?**

   ➢ It softens the cell walls, making it easier to squash the cells.

3. **Why is staining necessary for mitotic studies?**

   ➢ It helps to visualize the chromosomes clearly under a microscope.

Experiment 14: Stages of meiosis in *Tradescantia*, *Grasshopper testes*, or onion flower buds

Aim: To observe the stages of meiosis in Tradescantia, grasshopper testes, or onion flower buds.

Principle:

Meiosis is a type of cell division that reduces the chromosome number by half, leading to the formation of gametes. It consists of two successive divisions, meiosis I and meiosis II, and is crucial for genetic variation.

Preparation of Reagents:

1. **Fixative Solution:**
    a) Ethanol: Acetic acid (3:1)

2. **Acetocarmine Stain:**
    a) Acetocarmine - 1 g
    b) 45% Acetic acid - 100 mL

3. **1N Hydrochloric Acid (HCl):**
    a) Concentrated HCl - 8.3 mL
    b) Distilled water - up to 100 mL

Procedure:

1. Collect fresh flower buds or testes and fix them in fixative solution for 24 hours.

2. Rinse the sample and hydrolyze it in 1N HCl at 60°C for 10 minutes.

3. Stain the material with acetocarmine stain for 15 minutes.

4. Place a stained bud or testis on a slide, add a drop of water, and cover with a coverslip.

5. Gently press the coverslip to spread the cells and observe under a microscope.

Results:

Different stages of meiosis such as prophase I, metaphase I, anaphase I, and telophase I can be observed.

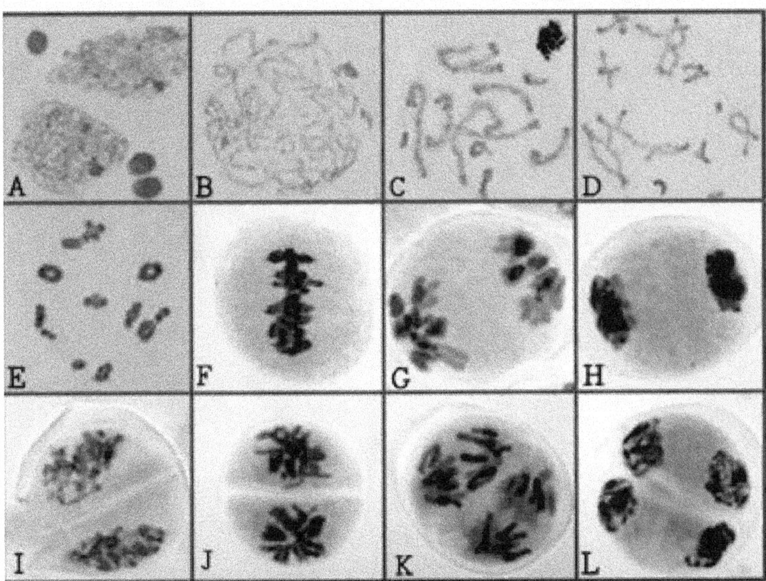

A-H : FIRST MEIOTIC CELL DIVISION STAGES (A-PROPHASE I (LEPTOTENE), B-PROPHASE I (ZYGOTENE), C-PROPHASE I (PACHYTENE), D-PROPHASE I (DIPLOTENE), E-PROPHASE I (DIAKINESIS), F-METAPHASE I (LATERAL VIEW), G-ANAPHASE I, H-TELOPHASE I)

I-L : SECOND MEIOTIC CELL DIVISION STAGES (I-PROPHASE II, J-METAPHASE II (POLAR VIEW), K-ANAPHASE II & L-TELOPHASE II)

Grasshopper testes

Discussion Questions and Answers:

1. **Why is meiosis important?**

    ➢ It ensures genetic variation and maintains chromosome number across generations.

2. **Why is staining necessary for observing meiosis?**

    ➢ It highlights chromosomes, making it easier to identify different stages.

Experiment 15: Cell Fractionation – Isolation of Mitochondria, Nucleus, and Cytosol

Aim: To isolate and study the cellular organelles - mitochondria, nucleus, and cytosol - using differential centrifugation.

Principle: Cell fractionation is a technique used to separate cellular organelles based on their size and density. It involves homogenization followed by differential centrifugation to sequentially isolate the nucleus, mitochondria, and cytosol.

Preparation of Reagents:

1. **Homogenization Buffer:**
   a) Sucrose - 0.25 M
   b) Tris-HCl (pH 7.4) - 50 mM
   c) EDTA - 1 mM
   d) Distilled water - up to 100 mL

2. **Centrifugation Buffer:**
   a) Sucrose - 0.25 M
   b) Tris-HCl (pH 7.4) - 50 mM
   c) $MgCl_2$ - 5 mM
   d) Distilled water - up to 100 mL

Procedure:

1. Homogenize the tissue sample in the homogenization buffer.
2. Centrifuge at 600 x g for 10 minutes to pellet the nuclei.
3. Transfer the supernatant and centrifuge at 10,000 x g for 20 minutes to pellet the mitochondria.

4. Transfer the supernatant again and centrifuge at 100,000 x g for 60 minutes to isolate the cytosol.

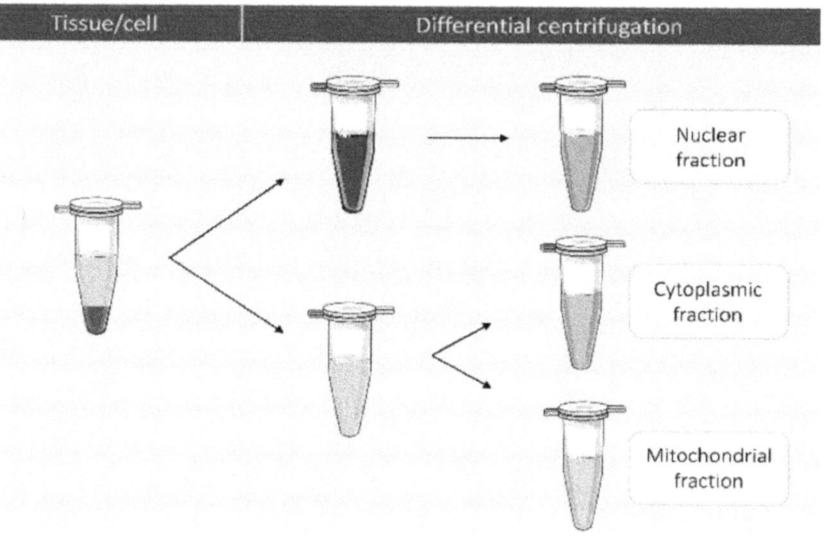

Results:

Nuclear, mitochondrial, and cytosolic fractions are obtained for further analysis.

Discussion Questions and Answers

1. **What is the purpose of cell fractionation?**
   - ➢ To isolate and study different organelles, such as the nucleus, mitochondria, and cytosol, for biochemical analysis.

2. **Why is sucrose used in the homogenization buffer?**
   - ➢ Sucrose helps to maintain osmotic balance and prevent the organelles from rupturing during homogenization.

3. **What is the principle of differential centrifugation?**

> It separates cellular components based on their size and density by applying increasing centrifugal forces.

4. **Why is it important to perform the isolation steps at low temperatures?**

> Low temperatures prevent enzymatic degradation and preserve the integrity of cellular organelles.

5. **How can you confirm the successful isolation of mitochondria?**

> By performing biochemical assays for mitochondrial enzymes such as succinate dehydrogenase.

Experiment 16: Staining of Mitochondria

Aim: To stain mitochondria in living cells to observe their structure and distribution.

Principle: Mitochondria can be stained using specific dyes that accumulate within them due to their membrane potential. Janus Green B is a commonly used dye that stains mitochondria blue-green.

Preparation of Reagents:

1. **Janus Green B Stain:**

   a) Janus Green B - 0.01% solution in distilled water

2. **Phosphate Buffer Solution (PBS):**

   a) Sodium chloride (NaCl) - 8 g

b) Potassium chloride (KCl) - 0.2 g

c) Sodium phosphate dibasic (Na_2HPO_4) - 1.44 g

d) Potassium phosphate monobasic (KH_2PO_4) - 0.24 g

e) Distilled water - up to 1 L

Procedure:

1. Prepare a slide with a drop of cell suspension.

2. Add a drop of Janus Green B stain and allow it to act for 2-3 minutes.

3. Rinse the slide gently with phosphate buffer solution.

4. Observe the slide under a microscope at 40x magnification.

Observation:

Mitochondria appear as blue-green structures within the cells.

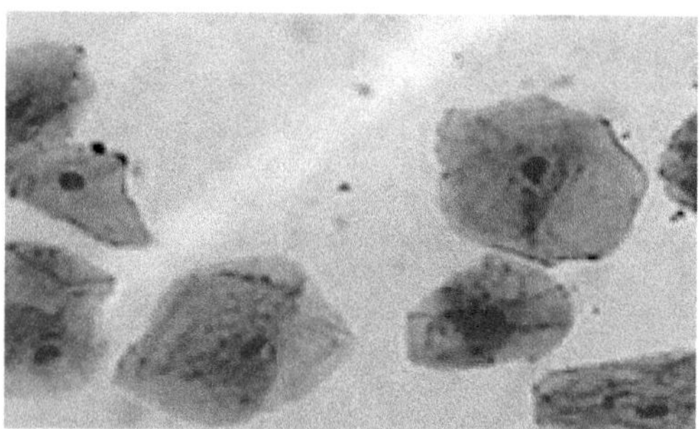

Discussion Questions and Answers:

1. **Why is Janus Green B used for mitochondrial staining?**

- o   It selectively stains mitochondria due to their oxidative activity.

2. **What is the role of the phosphate buffer in this experiment?**

   - o   It helps maintain the pH and prevent cellular damage during staining.

Experiment 17: To study the effect of plasmolysis and deplasmolysis in onion peel.

Aim: To observe the effect of plasmolysis and deplasmolysis in onion peel cells under a microscope.

Principle: Plasmolysis occurs when cells lose water in a hypertonic solution, causing the cytoplasm to shrink away from the cell wall. Deplasmolysis is the reverse process where cells regain water in a hypotonic solution.

Preparation of Reagents:

1. **Hypertonic Solution:** Prepare a 10% sodium chloride (NaCl) solution in distilled water.
2. **Hypotonic Solution:** Use distilled water for the experiment.

Procedure:

1. Peel a thin layer of onion skin and place it on a slide.
2. Add a few drops of hypertonic NaCl solution and observe under the microscope.
3. Record the plasmolysis effect as the cytoplasm shrinks.
4. Wash the slide with distilled water and add a few drops of distilled water.
5. Observe the cells under the microscope and record the deplasmolysis process.

Observation:

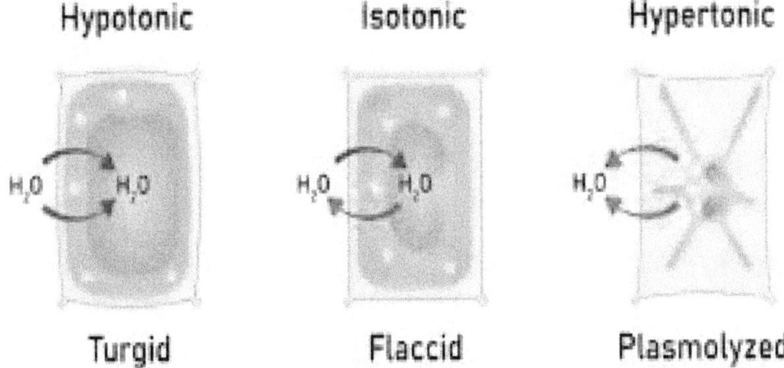

- In hypertonic solution: Cytoplasm shrinks and moves away from the cell wall.
- In hypotonic solution: Cytoplasm regains its original position.

Discussion Questions and Answers:

1. **Why does plasmolysis occur in onion cells?**
   - It occurs due to the movement of water out of the cell when placed in a hypertonic solution.

2. **What happens during deplasmolysis?**
   - Water re-enters the cell, restoring its turgor pressure.

3. **What is the importance of plasmolysis in plant cells?**
   - It helps in understanding osmoregulation and water movement in plant cells.

Experiment 18: Hypo and Hypertonic Effects on Erythrocytes

Aim: To study the effects of hypotonic and hypertonic solutions on erythrocytes.

Principle: Erythrocytes (red blood cells) undergo changes in shape and volume when placed in solutions of varying tonicity. In a hypotonic solution, water enters the cells causing them to swell and potentially burst (hemolysis), while in a hypertonic solution, water leaves the cells causing them to shrink (crenation).

Preparation of Reagents:

1. **Hypotonic Solution:**

   a) Prepare a 0.45% NaCl solution.

2. **Hypertonic Solution:**

   a) Prepare a 3% NaCl solution.

3. **Isotonic Solution:**

   a) Prepare a 0.9% NaCl solution.

Procedure:

1. Collect fresh blood sample and dilute with isotonic saline.
2. Divide into three test tubes, adding:
   - Hypotonic solution to the first.
   - Hypertonic solution to the second.
   - Isotonic solution to the third (control).
3. Incubate for 15 minutes and observe under the microscope.

Observation:

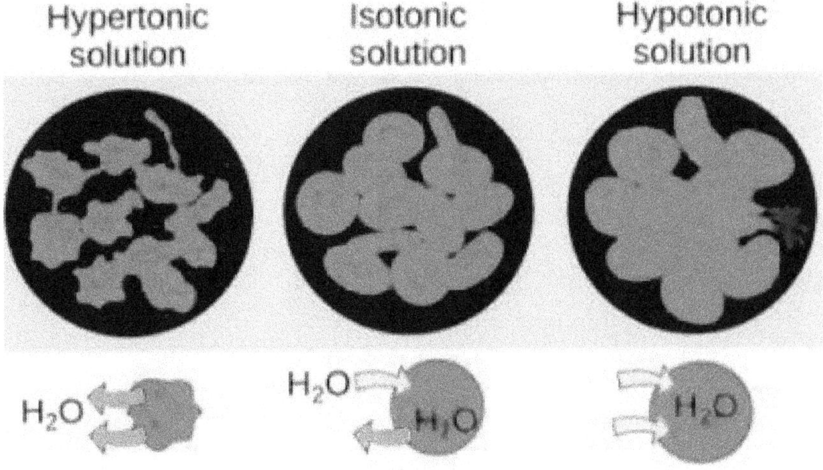

- Hypotonic: Cells swell and burst.

- Hypertonic: Cells shrink and become crenated.

- Isotonic: Cells retain their normal shape.

Discussion Questions and Answers:

1. **Why do erythrocytes burst in a hypotonic solution?**

   ➢ Due to the osmotic influx of water leading to cell lysis.

2. **What happens to erythrocytes in a hypertonic solution?**

   ➢ They lose water and shrink, forming crenated cells.

3. **Why is an isotonic solution used as a control?**

   ➢ To maintain normal cell morphology without osmotic effects

Experiment 19: Study of Different Types of Cells in the Human Blood Smear/Differential Cell Counting of Blood

Aim: To identify and count different types of cells in a human blood smear using staining techniques.

Principle: Blood smears are stained with differential stains, such as Wright's or Giemsa stain, to identify various blood cell types based on their morphology and staining properties.

Preparation of Reagents:

1. **Wright's Stain:**
   a) Wright's stain powder - 0.5 g
   b) Methanol - 100 mL
   c) Phosphate buffer (pH 6.8) - 100 mL

2. **Giemsa Stain:**
   a) Giemsa powder - 0.3 g
   b) Glycerol - 50 mL
   c) Methanol - 50 mL

Procedure:

1. Prepare a thin blood smear on a clean glass slide and air dry.
2. Fix the smear with methanol for 2 minutes.
3. Stain the slide with Wright's or Giemsa stain for 10 minutes.
4. Rinse with phosphate buffer and allow it to air dry.
5. Observe under the microscope and identify different blood cell types.

Observation:

- **Red Blood Cells (RBCs):** Biconcave, non-nucleated cells.
- **White Blood Cells (WBCs):** Various types including neutrophils, lymphocytes, monocytes, eosinophils, and basophils.
- **Platelets:** Small, irregularly shaped cell fragments involved in clotting.

Discussion Questions and Answers:

1. **Why is Wright's stain used for blood smears?**
   - It helps differentiate between different blood cells based on their staining properties.
2. **What is the significance of differential cell counting?**
   - It provides insight into health conditions such as infections, anemia, and leukemia.
3. **How can blood cell morphology indicate disease conditions?**
   - Abnormal shapes or sizes of cells can indicate conditions such as sickle cell anemia or leukemia

Experiment 20: Salivary Amylase Assay

Aim: To study the enzymatic activity of salivary amylase, determine its time kinetics, specific activity, and optimal temperature and pH, and investigate the effect of chloride ions on enzyme activity.

Principle: Salivary amylase catalyzes the breakdown of starch into maltose. The activity can be measured by monitoring the reduction in starch concentration using iodine and spectrophotometry.

Preparation of Reagents:

1. **Starch Solution (1% w/v):** Dissolve 1 g starch in 100 mL distilled water.
2. **Phosphate Buffer (pH 6.8):** Prepare using appropriate salts.
3. **Iodine Reagent:** Iodine - 0.01 N.
4. **Sodium Chloride Solution (0.5 M):** Dissolve NaCl in distilled water.

Procedure:

1. Prepare reaction mixtures with varying temperatures and pH.
2. Incubate starch solution with salivary amylase for different time intervals.
3. Add iodine reagent to stop the reaction and measure absorbance.
4. Determine the effect of NaCl by adding chloride ions to reaction mixtures.

Observation:

- Optimum temperature and pH conditions result in maximum enzyme activity.
- Higher NaCl concentrations may enhance or inhibit activity.

Discussion Questions and Answers:

1. **Why is pH important in enzyme activity?**
    - pH affects enzyme structure and function by altering active site conformation.
2. **How does temperature affect enzyme activity?**
    - Higher temperatures increase activity up to an optimum point beyond which denaturation occurs.
3. **What role do chloride ions play in salivary amylase activity?**
    - Chloride ions act as activators, enhancing enzymatic function.

Experiment 21: Mounting of Barr Bodies

Aim: To observe and identify Barr bodies in human epithelial cells.

Principle: Barr bodies are inactivated X chromosomes found in female somatic cells, appearing as dark-staining structures in the nucleus. They can be visualized using specific staining techniques such as Toluidine Blue.

Preparation of Reagents:

1. **Toluidine Blue Stain (0.1% w/v):**

    a) Toluidine blue - 0.1 g

    b) Distilled water - 100 mL

2. **Fixative Solution:**

    a) Ethanol: Acetic acid (3:1)

Procedure:

1. Collect buccal epithelial cells using a cotton swab.
2. Smear the cells onto a clean glass slide.
3. Fix the smear using the fixative solution for 5 minutes.
4. Stain the slide with Toluidine Blue for 2 minutes.
5. Rinse with distilled water and allow to air dry.
6. Observe under a microscope at 40x magnification.

Observation:

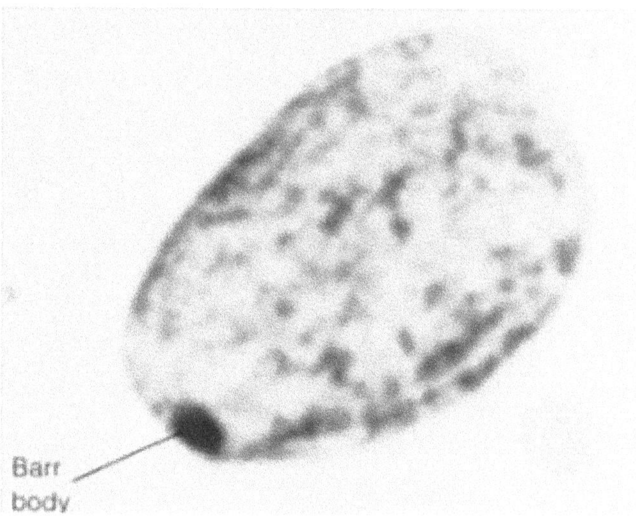

Barr bodies appear as dark-stained, round structures within the nucleus.

Discussion Questions and Answers:

1. **What is the significance of Barr bodies?**
   - Barr bodies indicate the presence of an inactive X chromosome in female cells.
2. **Why are Barr bodies not found in male cells?**
   - Males have only one X chromosome, which remains active.
3. **Which staining technique is commonly used for Barr body identification?**
   - Toluidine Blue staining is commonly used for its affinity to nuclear material.

Experiment 22: Study of Karyotyping in Onion and Humans (Normal and Abnormal)

Aim: To study karyotypes of onion root tip cells and human cells, including normal and abnormal karyotypes.

Principle: Karyotyping is a technique used to visualize chromosomes under a microscope to identify chromosomal abnormalities. In onion cells, karyotyping helps observe the diploid chromosome number, while in human cells, it aids in diagnosing genetic disorders.

Preparation of Reagents:

1. **Fixative Solution:**
   a) Ethanol: Acetic acid (3:1)

2. **Staining Solution:**

    a) Giemsa stain - 1% in phosphate buffer (pH 6.8)

Procedure:

1. Prepare onion root tips by fixing them in ethanol-acetic acid for 24 hours.
2. Stain the root tips with Giemsa stain for 10 minutes.
3. For human karyotyping, prepare a blood smear and fix with the fixative solution.
4. Stain the smear with Giemsa stain and examine under a microscope.

Observation:

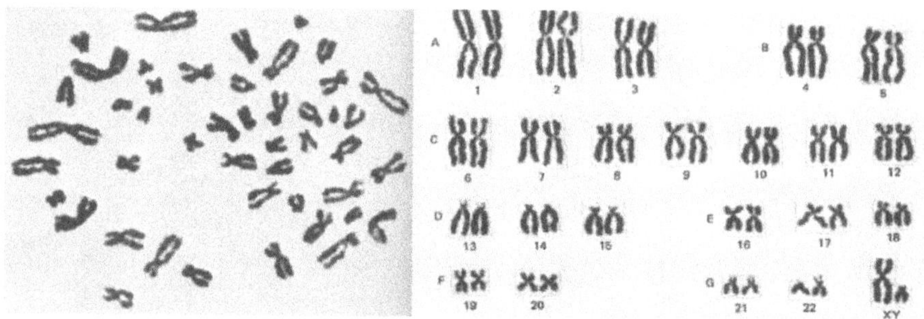

Human karyotypes can reveal normal (46 chromosomes) and abnormal (e.g., trisomy) conditions.

Discussion Questions and Answers:

1. **What is the significance of karyotyping?**

- o It helps in identifying chromosomal abnormalities and genetic disorders.

2. **Why is Giemsa stain used for karyotyping?**

   - o It provides clear banding patterns for chromosome identification.

3. **What are common abnormalities observed in human karyotypes?**

4. Conditions like Down syndrome (trisomy 21), Turner syndrome (45, X), and Klinefelter syndrome (47, XXY).

Experiment 23: Mounting of Polytene Chromosomes

Aim: To prepare and observe polytene chromosomes from salivary glands of Drosophila larvae.

Principle: Polytene chromosomes are large, multi-stranded chromosomes commonly found in the salivary glands of dipteran insects. They are useful for studying chromosomal structure and gene expression due to their distinct banding patterns.

Preparation of Reagents:

1. **Saline Solution (0.7% NaCl):**
   a) Dissolve 0.7 g of NaCl in 100 mL distilled water.
2. **Aceto-orcein Stain:**
   a) Dissolve 1 g orcein in 45% acetic acid.

Procedure:

1. Dissect salivary glands from third-instar Drosophila larvae in saline solution.
2. Transfer the glands onto a clean glass slide.
3. Add a drop of aceto-orcein stain and allow staining for 10 minutes.
4. Place a coverslip and gently squash the sample.
5. Observe under a microscope at 40x magnification.

Observation:

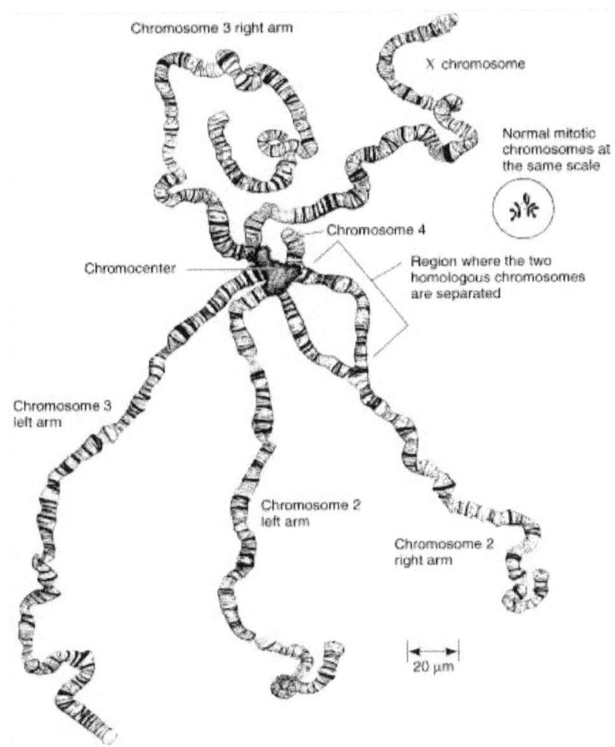

Polytene chromosomes appear as large, banded structures within the stained salivary gland cells.

Discussion Questions and Answers:

1. **What is the function of polytene chromosomes?**
   - They facilitate high levels of gene expression in certain tissues.
2. **Why are polytene chromosomes used in genetic studies?**
   - Their distinct banding pattern allows for the study of chromosomal structure and function.

3. **What is the significance of aceto-orcein staining?**

   o   It helps visualize chromosomal bands clearly under a microscope.

Experiment 24: DNA Isolation from Microorganisms

Aim: To isolate and purify DNA from microbial cells for further molecular analysis.

Principle: DNA isolation involves breaking the microbial cell wall

Lysis Buffer:

   a)   Tris-HCl (pH 8.0) - 50 mM

   b)   EDTA - 10 mM

   c)   SDS - 1%

Proteinase K Solution:

   a)   Proteinase K - 0.1 mg/mL

Phenol-Chloroform Solution:

   a)   Equal volumes of phenol, chloroform, and isoamyl alcohol (25:24:1)

Ethanol (70%):

   a)   Ethanol - 70% in distilled water

Procedure:

1. Harvest microbial cells by centrifuging the culture at 5000 rpm for 10 minutes.

2. Resuspend the cell pellet in lysis buffer and incubate at 37°C for 30 minutes.

3. Add Proteinase K and incubate at 55°C for 1 hour to digest proteins.

4. Add an equal volume of phenol-chloroform solution and mix by gentle inversion.

5. Centrifuge at 10,000 rpm for 10 minutes to separate phases.

6. Carefully transfer the upper aqueous phase containing DNA to a fresh tube.

7. Add cold ethanol and incubate at -20°C for 30 minutes to precipitate DNA.

8. Centrifuge at 10,000 rpm for 10 minutes to collect the DNA pellet.

9. Wash the pellet with 70% ethanol and air dry.

10. Resuspend the DNA pellet in TE buffer for storage.

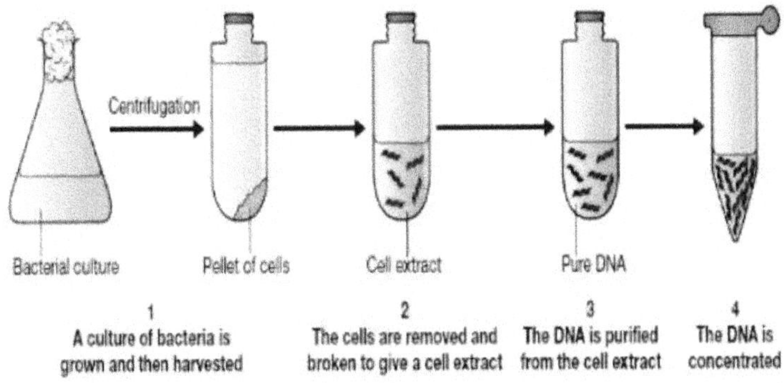

Results:

A visible DNA pellet should be obtained at the bottom of the tube, which can be quantified and analyzed further.

Discussion Questions and Answers:

1. **Why is Proteinase K used in DNA isolation?**
   - It helps to degrade proteins and remove contaminants from the sample.
2. **What is the role of phenol-chloroform in DNA extraction?**
   - It separates DNA from proteins and other cellular debris.
3. **Why is cold ethanol used for DNA precipitation?**
   - It helps to concentrate and visualize the DNA pellet.
4. **What precautions should be taken during DNA isolation?**
   - Use sterile equipment and avoid contamination to ensure sample purity

Experiment 25 : Isolation of DNA from Plant Source

Aim: To isolate and purify DNA from plant tissues for molecular biology applications.

Principle: DNA isolation from plant sources involves breaking down the cell wall, membrane, and organelles to release DNA. Plant tissues contain polysaccharides and secondary metabolites that require specialized buffers to remove impurities effectively.

Preparation of Reagents:

1. **Extraction Buffer:**
    a) Tris-HCl (pH 8.0) - 100 mM
    b) EDTA - 25 mM
    c) NaCl - 1.5 M
    d) CTAB - 2%
2. **Chloroform-Isoamyl Alcohol (24:1):**
    a) Chloroform - 24 parts
    b) Isoamyl alcohol - 1 part
3. **Isopropanol (100%)**
4. **Ethanol (70%)**
5. **RNase Solution:** RNase A - 10 mg/mL

Procedure:

1. Collect fresh plant tissue (about 1 g), wash with distilled water, and grind in liquid nitrogen to a fine powder.

2. Add 5 mL of extraction buffer and incubate at 65°C for 30 minutes with occasional mixing.

3. Add an equal volume of chloroform-isoamyl alcohol (24:1), mix gently, and centrifuge at 10,000 rpm for 10 minutes.

4. Transfer the aqueous phase to a fresh tube and add RNase solution, incubate at 37°C for 30 minutes.

5. Precipitate the DNA by adding an equal volume of isopropanol and incubate at -20°C for 30 minutes.

6. Centrifuge at 10,000 rpm for 10 minutes to collect the DNA pellet.

7. Wash the pellet with 70% ethanol, air dry, and dissolve in TE buffer.

Results:

A visible white DNA pellet is obtained at the bottom of the tube, which can be further analyzed for purity and concentration.

Discussion Questions and Answers:

1. **Why is CTAB used in plant DNA extraction?**
   - ➤ CTAB helps remove polysaccharides and secondary metabolites that interfere with DNA purity.

2. **What is the purpose of using RNase in DNA extraction?**
   - ➤ RNase degrades RNA contamination, ensuring pure DNA samples.

3. **Why is liquid nitrogen used during grinding?**

> It prevents enzymatic degradation and preserves DNA integrity by rapid freezing.

4. **What is the role of isopropanol in DNA precipitation?**

> Isopropanol helps precipitate DNA by reducing its solubility in the solution.

Experiment 26: DNA Isolation from Animal Source

Aim: To isolate and purify DNA from animal tissues for molecular biology applications.

Principle: DNA isolation from animal sources involves breaking the cell membrane and nuclear envelope to release DNA. Protein digestion and precipitation steps are necessary to remove cellular proteins and other contaminants.

Preparation of Reagents:

1. **Lysis Buffer:**
     a) Tris-HCl (pH 8.0) - 100 mM
     b) EDTA - 25 mM
     c) SDS - 1%
2. **Proteinase K Solution:**
     a) Proteinase K - 0.1 mg/mL
3. **Phenol-Chloroform-Isoamyl Alcohol (25:24:1):**
     a) Phenol - 25 parts
     b) Chloroform - 24 parts
     c) Isoamyl alcohol - 1 part
4. **Isopropanol (100%)**
5. **Ethanol (70%)**
6. **RNase Solution:** RNase A - 10 mg/mL

Procedure:

1. Collect animal tissue (about 1 g) and homogenize in lysis buffer.

2. Incubate the homogenate at 55°C for 1 hour with Proteinase K to digest proteins.

3. Add an equal volume of phenol-chloroform-isoamyl alcohol and mix gently.

4. Centrifuge at 10,000 rpm for 10 minutes to separate the phases.

5. Carefully transfer the upper aqueous phase to a fresh tube.

6. Treat with RNase solution and incubate at 37°C for 30 minutes.

7. Precipitate the DNA by adding an equal volume of isopropanol and incubate at -20°C for 30 minutes.

8. Centrifuge at 10,000 rpm for 10 minutes to collect the DNA pellet.

9. Wash the pellet with 70% ethanol, air dry, and dissolve in TE buffer.

Results:

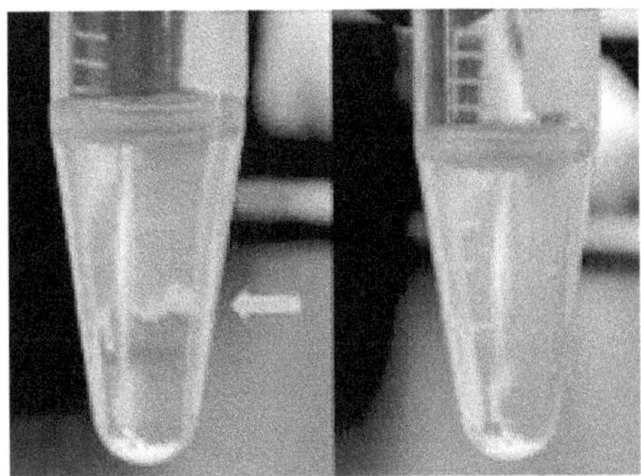

A visible white DNA pellet is obtained, which can be further analyzed for purity and concentration.

Discussion Questions and Answers:

1. **Why is Proteinase K used in DNA extraction from animal tissues?**

   It helps to degrade proteins and remove contaminants from the sample.

2. **What is the purpose of using phenol-chloroform in DNA extraction?**

   It separates DNA from proteins and other cellular debris.

3. **Why is isopropanol used for DNA precipitation?**

   Isopropanol reduces DNA solubility, allowing it to precipitate out of the solution.

4. **What precautions should be taken during DNA isolation?**

   Use sterile equipment and avoid contamination to ensure sample purity.

Experiment 27: DNA Estimation – Spectrophotometric Method

Aim: To estimate the concentration of DNA in a given sample using a spectrophotometer.

Principle: DNA absorbs ultraviolet (UV) light at a wavelength of 260 nm due to the presence of nucleotide bases. The concentration of DNA in a solution can be determined by measuring its absorbance at 260 nm, and the purity can be assessed using the A260/A280 ratio, where a ratio of ~1.8 indicates pure DNA.

Preparation of Reagents:

1. **TE Buffer (pH 8.0):**
    a) Tris-HCl - 10 mM
    b) EDTA - 1 mM
    c) Distilled water - up to 100 mL

2. **DNA Standard Solution:**
    a) Prepare a stock solution of known DNA concentration.

Procedure:

1. Prepare DNA sample by diluting it in TE buffer.
2. Blank the spectrophotometer with TE buffer at 260 nm.
3. Measure the absorbance of the DNA sample at 260 nm and 280 nm.
4. Calculate the concentration using the formula:

5. Assess the purity of DNA by calculating the A260/A280 ratio.

Results:

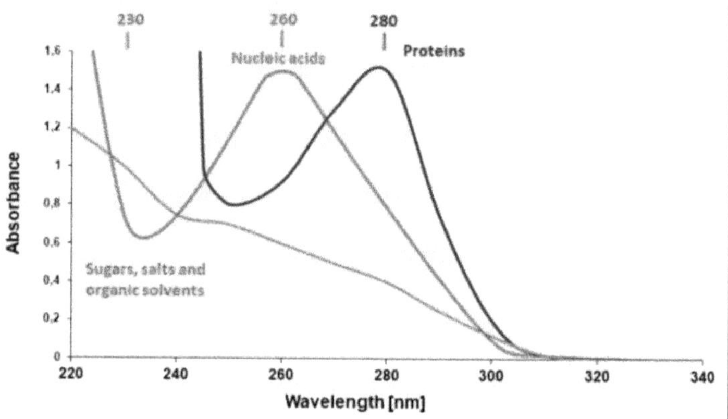

The concentration of DNA is calculated using the absorbance readings. A ratio of ~1.8 indicates pure DNA, while a lower ratio suggests protein contamination.

Discussion Questions and Answers:

1. **Why is absorbance measured at 260 nm for DNA estimation?**

   ➢ DNA absorbs UV light at 260 nm due to the presence of purine and pyrimidine bases.

2. **What does the A260/A280 ratio indicate?**

   ➢ It indicates the purity of DNA, with a ratio of ~1.8 being considered pure.

3. **How can protein contamination be detected in DNA samples?**

> If the A260/A280 ratio is lower than 1.8, it indicates protein contamination.

4. **Why is TE buffer used in DNA estimation?**

> TE buffer helps maintain the stability and integrity of DNA during spectrophotometric analysis.

Experiment 28: Isolation of Plasmid DNA from bacterial cell

Aim: To isolate plasmid DNA from bacterial cells for further molecular biology applications.

Principle: Plasmids are small, circular, double-stranded DNA molecules that replicate independently of chromosomal DNA. The isolation process involves cell lysis, plasmid DNA separation from chromosomal DNA and proteins, and precipitation for further analysis.

Preparation of Reagents:

1. **Alkaline Lysis Buffer (Solution I):**
   a) Tris-HCl (pH 8.0) - 50 mM
   b) EDTA - 10 mM
   c) Glucose - 25 mM

a) **Lysis Buffer (Solution II):**
   a. NaOH - 0.2 N
   b. SDS - 1%

2. **Neutralization Buffer (Solution III):**
   a) Potassium acetate - 3 M
   b) Glacial acetic acid - 5 M

3. **Isopropanol (100%)**

4. **Ethanol (70%)**

Procedure:

1. Harvest bacterial culture by centrifuging at 6000 rpm for 10 minutes.

2. Resuspend the pellet in Solution I and incubate on ice for 5 minutes.

3. Add Solution II, mix gently by inverting, and incubate on ice for 5 minutes.

4. Add Solution III and incubate on ice for 10 minutes.

5. Centrifuge at 10,000 rpm for 15 minutes to separate plasmid DNA.

6. Transfer the supernatant to a fresh tube and add an equal volume of isopropanol.

7. Incubate at -20°C for 30 minutes and centrifuge at 12,000 rpm for 10 minutes.

8. Wash the pellet with 70% ethanol, air dry, and dissolve in TE buffer.

Results:

A visible plasmid DNA pellet should be obtained, which can be analyzed by gel electrophoresis.

Discussion Questions and Answers:

1. **Why is SDS used in plasmid isolation?**
    - ➤ SDS helps lyse bacterial cells by disrupting the lipid bilayer and denaturing proteins.

2. **What is the purpose of potassium acetate in Solution III?**
    - ➤ It neutralizes the alkaline lysate and precipitates cellular debris.

3. **Why is isopropanol used for DNA precipitation?**

> ➤ Isopropanol reduces DNA solubility, allowing it to precipitate out of the solution.

4. **How can the purity of isolated plasmid DNA be assessed?**

> ➤ By measuring the A260/A280 ratio in a spectrophotometer.

Experiment 29: Bacterial Transformation

Aim: To introduce foreign DNA into a bacterial cell and analyze its expression.

Principle: Bacterial transformation is the process by which bacteria take up foreign DNA from their surroundings. Competent bacterial cells are prepared to allow DNA uptake, and successful transformation is analyzed by selecting for antibiotic resistance or expressing a marker gene.

Preparation of Reagents:

1. **Competent Cell Preparation Solution:**
   a) Calcium chloride ($CaCl_2$) - 50 mM
   b) Tris-HCl (pH 7.5) - 10 mM

2. **Luria-Bertani (LB) Agar Plates:**
   a) Tryptone - 10 g
   b) Yeast extract - 5 g
   c) NaCl - 10 g
   d) Agar - 15 g
   e) Distilled water - up to 1 L

3. **Antibiotic Solution:**
   a) Ampicillin - 100 µg/mL

4. **Plasmid DNA Solution:** Prepared plasmid containing an antibiotic resistance gene.

Procedure:

1. Prepare competent bacterial cells by suspending in CaCl$_2$ solution and incubating on ice.

2. Add the plasmid DNA to the competent cells and incubate on ice for 30 minutes.

3. Heat-shock the cells at 42°C for 45 seconds to facilitate DNA uptake.

4. Incubate the cells on ice for 2 minutes.

5. Add LB broth and incubate at 37°C for 1 hour to allow gene expression.

6. Spread the transformed cells onto LB agar plates containing the antibiotic.

7. Incubate overnight at 37°C and observe colony formation.

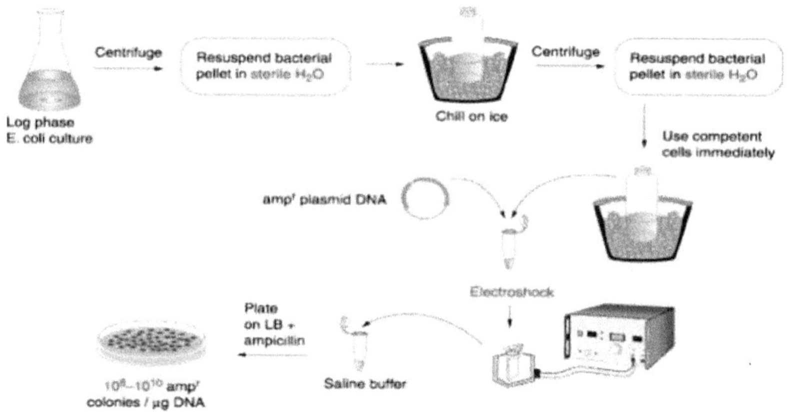

Results:

Successful transformation is indicated by the growth of bacterial colonies on antibiotic-containing plates.

Discussion Questions and Answers:

1. **Why is calcium chloride used in bacterial transformation?**

   It increases cell membrane permeability, facilitating DNA uptake.

2. **What is the purpose of the heat shock step?**

   Heat shock induces a thermal imbalance that drives DNA into the cells.

3. **How is successful transformation confirmed?**

   By observing colony growth on selective media containing an antibiotic.

4. **What factors influence transformation efficiency?**

   Factors such as DNA concentration, cell competence, and incubation conditions.

Experiment 30: Gene Cloning

Aim: To clone a specific gene of interest into a plasmid vector and introduce it into a host organism for expression.

Principle: Gene cloning involves inserting a target gene into a plasmid vector using restriction enzymes and DNA ligase, followed by transformation into a host organism such as E. coli. The host cells are then screened for the presence of recombinant plasmids.

Preparation of Reagents:

1. **Restriction Enzyme Digestion Buffer:**
   a) Tris-HCl (pH 7.5) - 50 mM
   b) $MgCl_2$ - 10 mM

2. **Ligation Buffer:**
   a) ATP - 1 mM
   b) DNA ligase - 1 U/mL

3. **Competent Cells Solution:**
   a) Calcium chloride ($CaCl_2$) - 50 mM

Procedure:

1. Digest the plasmid vector and target DNA with restriction enzymes.
2. Mix the digested DNA with ligation buffer and DNA ligase.
3. Incubate the ligation reaction at 16°C overnight.
4. Transform the recombinant plasmid into competent cells.
5. Plate the transformed cells on selective LB agar plates.
6. Incubate overnight at 37°C and analyze the colonies.

Results: Successful gene cloning is confirmed by the growth of recombinant colonies on selective media.

Discussion Questions and Answers:

1. **Why are restriction enzymes used in gene cloning?**

    To create specific sites for inserting the gene into the plasmid.

2. **What is the role of DNA ligase in cloning?**

    It joins the target gene with the plasmid vector.

3. **How is successful cloning confirmed?**

    Through colony PCR or restriction digestion analysis.

Experiment 31: Digestion of DNA using Restriction Enzymes and Analysis by Agarose Gel Electrophoresis

Aim: To digest DNA with restriction enzymes and analyze the digested fragments using agarose gel electrophoresis.

Principle: Restriction enzymes, also known as restriction endonucleases, recognize specific sequences in DNA and cut at or near these sites. The resulting DNA fragments can be separated based on their size using agarose gel electrophoresis, which allows visualization and analysis of DNA.

Preparation of Reagents:

1. **Restriction Enzyme Digestion Buffer:**
    a) Tris-HCl (pH 7.5) - 50 mM
    b) $MgCl_2$ - 10 mM
    c) NaCl - 100 mM

2. **Agarose Gel Solution:**
    a) Agarose - 1.0% w/v
    b) TAE buffer (1X)

3. **DNA Loading Dye:**
    a) Bromophenol blue - 0.25%
    b) Xylene cyanol - 0.25%
    c) Glycerol - 50%

4. **Ethidium Bromide Solution:**
    a) Ethidium bromide - 0.5 μg/mL

5. **DNA Sample:**
    a) Plasmid or genomic DNA

Procedure:

1. Prepare the digestion reaction by adding DNA, restriction enzyme, and digestion buffer.
2. Incubate the reaction mixture at the optimal temperature (usually 37°C) for 1-2 hours.
3. Prepare a 1% agarose gel by dissolving agarose in TAE buffer and cooling to 50°C.
4. Add ethidium bromide to the agarose gel and pour into the gel casting tray.
5. Load digested DNA samples mixed with loading dye into the gel wells.
6. Run electrophoresis at 80-100V for 45-60 minutes.
7. Visualize the DNA bands under UV light and analyze the fragment sizes.

Results:

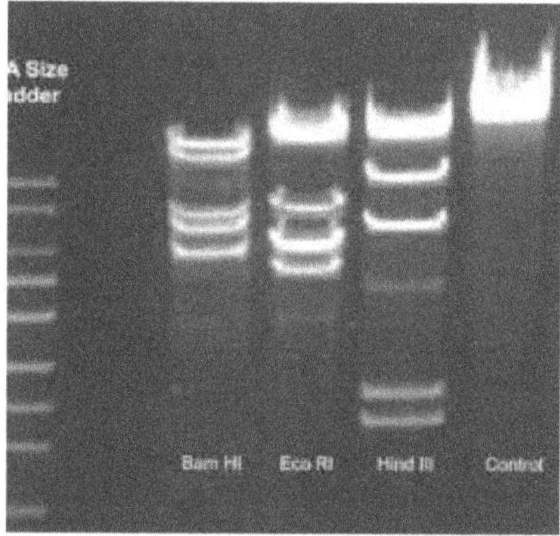

The DNA fragments appear as distinct bands under UV light, with their migration based on molecular weight.

Discussion Questions and Answers:

1. **Why are restriction enzymes used in DNA digestion?**

   They cut DNA at specific recognition sites, allowing for the analysis and manipulation of DNA.

2. **What is the purpose of agarose gel electrophoresis?**

   It separates DNA fragments based on their size.

3. **Why is ethidium bromide used in gel electrophoresis?**

   It intercalates with DNA and fluoresces under UV light, allowing visualization.

4. **What factors influence the migration of DNA in an agarose gel?**

   Factors such as gel concentration, voltage applied, and DNA fragment size.

Experiment 32: Isolation of RNA from Cells

Aim: To isolate and purify RNA from cells for molecular biology applications.

Principle: RNA isolation involves breaking down the cell membrane and organelles to release RNA while preventing degradation by ribonucleases (RNases). The process typically involves cell lysis, phase separation using organic solvents, and RNA precipitation.

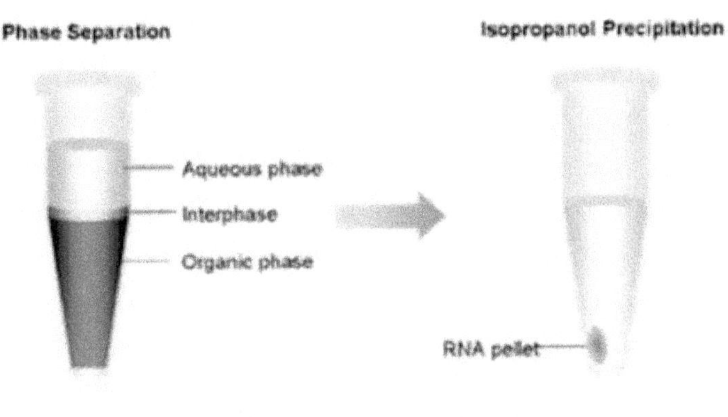

RNA Isolation Principle

Preparation of Reagents:

1. **Lysis Buffer:**
   a) Tris-HCl (pH 8.0) - 50 mM
   b) EDTA - 10 mM
   c) SDS - 1%

2. **Phenol-Chloroform-Isoamyl Alcohol (25:24:1):**
   a) Phenol - 25 parts
   b) Chloroform - 24 parts

c) Isoamyl alcohol - 1 part

3. **Isopropanol (100%)**
4. **Ethanol (70%)**
5. **RNase-Free Water**

Procedure:

1. Collect the cells and homogenize in lysis buffer to break open the cells.
2. Add an equal volume of phenol-chloroform-isoamyl alcohol and mix well.
3. Centrifuge the mixture at 12,000 rpm for 10 minutes to separate the phases.
4. Carefully transfer the upper aqueous phase containing RNA to a fresh tube.
5. Precipitate RNA by adding an equal volume of isopropanol and incubating at -20°C for 30 minutes.
6. Centrifuge at 12,000 rpm for 15 minutes to collect the RNA pellet.
7. Wash the pellet with 70% ethanol, air dry, and resuspend in RNase-free water.

Results:

A visible RNA pellet should be obtained, which can be quantified using spectrophotometry or electrophoresis.

Discussion Questions and Answers:

1. **Why is phenol-chloroform used in RNA isolation?**
   - It helps in phase separation, allowing RNA to remain in the aqueous phase while proteins and DNA are removed.

2. **What precautions are necessary during RNA isolation?**
   - Use RNase-free reagents and wear gloves to prevent contamination.

3. **Why is isopropanol used for RNA precipitation?**
   - It helps concentrate the RNA by reducing its solubility.

4. **What is the role of EDTA in the lysis buffer?**
   - EDTA chelates divalent cations and inhibits RNase activity, protecting the RNA.

Experiment 33: Polymerase Chain Reaction (PCR)

Aim: To amplify specific DNA sequences using the polymerase chain reaction (PCR) technique.

Principle: PCR is a molecular biology technique used to amplify a specific DNA sequence exponentially through cycles of denaturation, annealing, and extension using a thermostable DNA polymerase.

Preparation of Reagents:

a) **PCR Reaction Mixture:**
   a. Template DNA - 10-50 ng
   b. Forward Primer - 10 μM
   c. Reverse Primer - 10 μM
   d. dNTP Mix - 200 μM each
   e. Taq DNA Polymerase - 1.25 U
   f. PCR Buffer (10X) - 1X final concentration
   g. $MgCl_2$ - 1.5-2.5 mM
   h. Nuclease-free water - up to final volume (usually 25-50 μL)

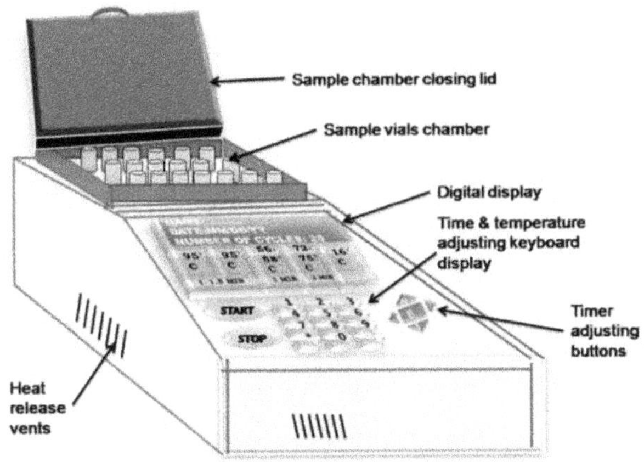

PCR Machine

b) Agarose Gel for Electrophoresis:

a) Agarose - 1-2%

b) 1X TAE or TBE buffer

c) Ethidium bromide or SYBR Green stain

Procedure:

1. Prepare the PCR reaction mixture by adding all components in a sterile PCR tube.

2. Place the tubes in a thermal cycler and set the following cycling conditions:

   - **Initial Denaturation:** 94°C for 3 minutes

   - **Denaturation:** 94°C for 30 seconds

   - **Annealing:** 50-65°C for 30 seconds (temperature depends on primer Tm)

- o **Extension:** 72°C for 1 minute per kb of target DNA
- o **Final Extension:** 72°C for 5 minutes
- o **Number of Cycles:** 30-35

3. Run the amplified DNA on agarose gel electrophoresis to verify the amplification.

4. Visualize the bands under UV light.

Results:

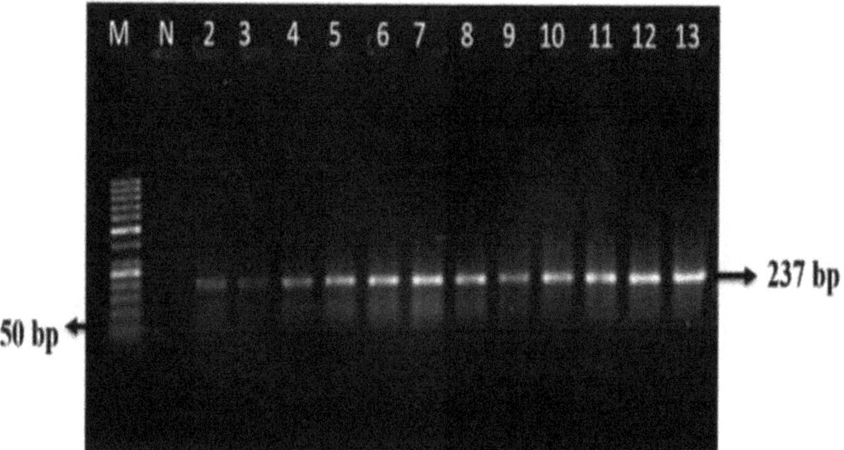

Successful amplification results in the presence of distinct DNA bands of the expected size.

Discussion Questions and Answers:

1. **What is the purpose of PCR?**
   - o PCR is used to amplify specific DNA sequences for various applications such as cloning, sequencing, and diagnostics.

2. **Why is Taq DNA polymerase used in PCR?**

- o Taq polymerase is heat-stable and can withstand the high temperatures of the denaturation step.

3. **What factors affect the efficiency of PCR?**

   - o Primer design, annealing temperature, magnesium concentration, and template quality.

4. **What is the purpose of the annealing step in PCR?**

   - o It allows the primers to bind to the complementary DNA sequence.

5. **Why is gel electrophoresis used after PCR?**

   - o To confirm the presence and size of the amplified DNA fragments.

Experiment 34: Determination of Blood Groups - Slide Agglutination Test

Aim: To determine the blood group of an individual using the slide agglutination test.

Principle: Blood grouping is based on the presence or absence of specific antigens (A and B) on the surface of red blood cells. When anti-A or anti-B antibodies are mixed with a blood sample, agglutination (clumping) occurs if the corresponding antigen is present.

Preparation of Reagents:

1. **Anti-A Serum:**
   a) Contains antibodies against A antigen
2. **Anti-B Serum:**
   a) Contains antibodies against B antigen
3. **Anti-D Serum (Rh factor):**
   a) Contains antibodies against Rh antigen
4. **Normal Saline (0.9% NaCl Solution)**

Procedure:

1. Place a drop of anti-A serum, anti-B serum, and anti-D serum separately on a clean glass slide.
2. Add a small drop of blood sample to each drop of serum.
3. Mix gently with a glass rod and observe for agglutination.
4. Interpret the results based on the presence or absence of agglutination.

	Group A	Group B	Group AB	Group O
Red blood cell type	A	B	AB	O
Antibodies in plasma	Anti-B	Anti-A	None	Anti-A and Anti-B
Antigens in red blood cell	A antigen	B antigen	A and B antigens	None

Results:

- **Blood Group A:** Agglutination with anti-A serum, no reaction with anti-B serum.
- **Blood Group B:** Agglutination with anti-B serum, no reaction with anti-A serum.
- **Blood Group AB:** Agglutination with both anti-A and anti-B sera.
- **Blood Group O:** No agglutination with either anti-A or anti-B sera.
- **Rh Positive:** Agglutination with anti-D serum.
- **Rh Negative:** No agglutination with anti-D serum.

Discussion Questions and Answers:

1. **What causes agglutination in the slide agglutination test?**
   - The interaction between specific antigens on red blood cells and their corresponding antibodies.

2. **Why is normal saline used in the test?**

   o It helps maintain isotonic conditions and prevents hemolysis.

3. **What does a positive Rh factor indicate?**

   o It indicates the presence of the Rh (D) antigen on red blood cells.

4. **Why is blood grouping important?**

   o It is crucial for blood transfusions, organ transplantation, and pregnancy management.

Experiment 35: Immuno-Precipitation

Aim: To isolate and analyze specific proteins from a complex mixture using the immuno-precipitation technique.

Principle: Immuno-precipitation is a technique that utilizes the specific binding of an antibody to its antigen to isolate target proteins from a mixture. The antigen-antibody complex is then precipitated using Protein A/G beads, allowing for further analysis through techniques such as SDS-PAGE or Western blotting.

Preparation of Reagents:

1. **Lysis Buffer:**
    a) Tris-HCl (pH 7.5) - 50 mM
    b) NaCl - 150 mM
    c) NP-40 - 1%
    d) EDTA - 1 mM

2. **Antibody Solution:**
    a) Specific primary antibody against the target protein

3. **Protein A/G Beads:**
    a) Pre-washed magnetic or agarose beads

4. **Wash Buffer:**
    a) Tris-HCl (pH 7.5) - 50 mM
    b) NaCl - 150 mM

5. **Elution Buffer:**
    a) Glycine-HCl (pH 2.8) - 100 mM

Procedure:

1. Lyse the cells using lysis buffer and centrifuge to remove debris.
2. Incubate the lysate with the specific antibody and gently rotate for 1-2 hours at 4°C.
3. Add Protein A/G beads to the mixture and incubate for an additional hour at 4°C.
4. Wash the beads three times with wash buffer to remove non-specific binding.
5. Elute the bound protein using elution buffer.
6. Analyze the eluted protein by SDS-PAGE or Western blotting or Microarray

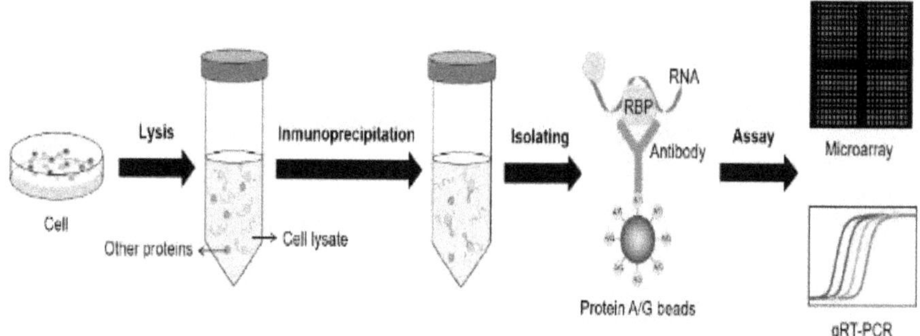

Results:

A specific protein band should be detected in the analysis, confirming successful immuno-precipitation.

Discussion Questions and Answers:

1. **What is the purpose of using Protein A/G beads?**
   - They bind to the Fc region of antibodies, facilitating the precipitation of antigen-antibody complexes.
2. **Why is lysis buffer used in immuno-precipitation?**
   - It helps in breaking the cell membrane to release target proteins into solution.
3. **What factors influence the efficiency of immuno-precipitation?**
   - Factors such as antibody specificity, incubation time, and bead quality.
4. **What downstream applications can be performed after immuno-precipitation?**
   - SDS-PAGE, Western blotting, or mass spectrometry for protein analysis

Experiment 36: Ouchterlony Double Diffusion

Aim: To analyze antigen-antibody interactions using the Ouchterlony double diffusion technique.

Principle: Ouchterlony double diffusion is a qualitative immunodiffusion technique used to detect and compare antigens and antibodies based on their diffusion in an agar medium. When antigens and antibodies diffuse towards each other, they form a visible precipitin line if they are specific to each other.

Preparation of Reagents:

1. **Agar Gel:**
   a) Agarose - 1%
   b) Phosphate-buffered saline (PBS) - 1X

2. **Antibody Solution:**
   a) Specific antibodies against the target antigen

3. **Antigen Solution:**
   a) Purified antigen sample

4. **Staining Solution:**
   a) Coomassie Brilliant Blue or Amido Black for visualization

Procedure:

1. Prepare a 1% agarose gel in PBS and pour it onto a glass plate.
2. Cut wells into the agar using a template.

3. Load the central well with the antibody solution and the surrounding wells with antigen samples.

4. Incubate the plate in a moist chamber at room temperature for 24-48 hours to allow diffusion.

5. Observe the formation of precipitin lines indicating antigen-antibody interactions.

6. Stain the gel for better visualization if needed.

Results:

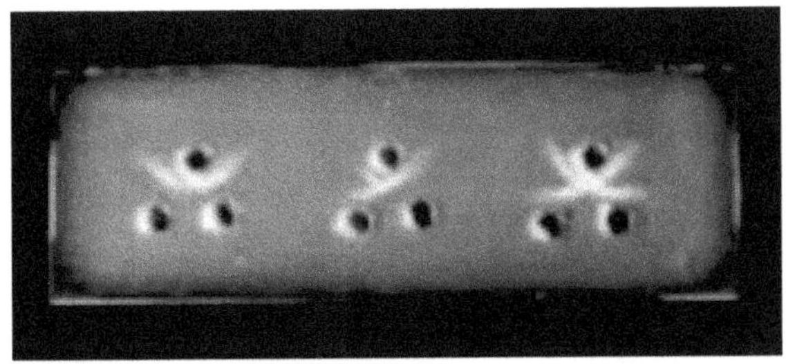

Visible precipitin lines indicate a positive antigen-antibody reaction, confirming the presence and specificity of the antigen.

Discussion Questions and Answers:

1. **What is the significance of Ouchterlony double diffusion?**
    - It helps in identifying and comparing antigen-antibody interactions.

2. **Why is agarose used in the gel preparation?**
    - Agarose provides a suitable medium for antigen and antibody diffusion.

3. **What do precipitin lines indicate in this test?**

   - They indicate the formation of antigen-antibody complexes.

4. **How can cross-reactivity be detected in Ouchterlony double diffusion?**

   - If different antigens share epitopes, they may form spur formation in precipitin lines.

Experiment 37: Enzyme-Linked Immunosorbent Assay (ELISA)

Aim: To detect and quantify specific proteins or antigens using the ELISA technique.

Principle: ELISA is an immunological technique that uses antigen-antibody interactions to detect the presence of specific biomolecules. The assay is based on the immobilization of antigens or antibodies onto a solid surface, followed by enzyme-conjugated secondary antibodies that produce a measurable color change upon the addition of a substrate.

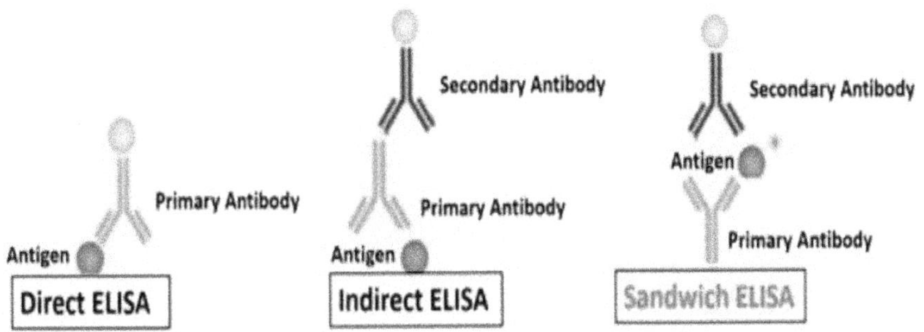

Preparation of Reagents:

1. **Coating Buffer:**
     a) Carbonate-bicarbonate buffer (pH 9.6)

2. **Blocking Solution:**
     a) 1% Bovine Serum Albumin (BSA) in PBS

3. **Primary Antibody Solution:**
     a) Specific antibody diluted in PBS

4. **Secondary Antibody Solution:**

a) Enzyme-conjugated antibody (HRP or ALP)

5. **Substrate Solution:**

    a) TMB (Tetramethylbenzidine) for HRP or pNPP for ALP

6. **Stop Solution:**

    a) 1N Sulfuric acid (for HRP) or 3N NaOH (for ALP)

Procedure:

1. Coat a 96-well ELISA plate with antigen diluted in coating buffer and incubate overnight at 4°C.
2. Wash the wells with PBS containing 0.05% Tween-20 (PBST) to remove unbound antigen.
3. Block the wells with blocking solution for 1 hour at room temperature.
4. Add the primary antibody and incubate for 1-2 hours at room temperature.
5. Wash the plate thoroughly to remove unbound antibodies.
6. Add the enzyme-conjugated secondary antibody and incubate for 1 hour.
7. Wash the plate and add the substrate solution.
8. Incubate until a color change is observed, then stop the reaction with the stop solution.
9. Measure absorbance at the appropriate wavelength (e.g., 450 nm for TMB).

Results:

The intensity of the color developed is proportional to the concentration of the antigen present in the sample and is measured using a microplate reader.

Discussion Questions and Answers:

1. **What is the purpose of the blocking step in ELISA?**
   - To prevent non-specific binding and reduce background noise.
2. **How does the enzyme-substrate reaction produce a measurable signal?**
   - The enzyme catalyzes a colorimetric reaction that can be quantified using a spectrophotometer.
3. **What are the different types of ELISA?**
   - Direct, indirect, sandwich, and competitive ELISA.
4. **Why is ELISA used in clinical diagnostics?**
   - It provides high sensitivity and specificity for detecting diseases such as HIV, hepatitis, and autoimmune disorders.

Experiment 38: Aseptic Transfer Techniques

Aim: To learn and practice aseptic techniques to prevent contamination during microbial transfer.

Principle: Aseptic techniques are essential to maintain the sterility of cultures and equipment, ensuring accurate results in microbiological studies by preventing the introduction of unwanted microorganisms.

Procedure:

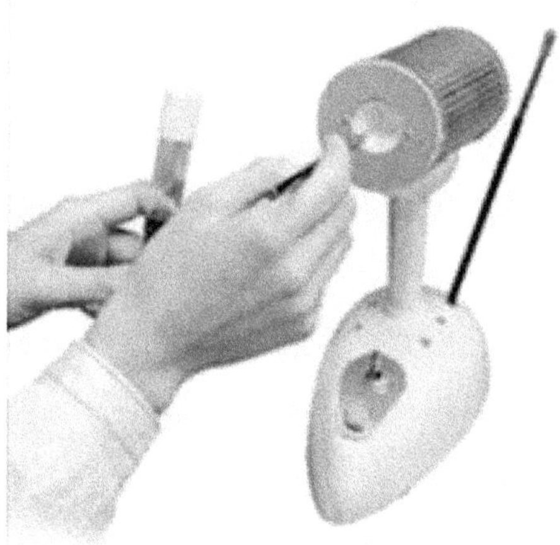

1. Sterilize inoculating loops and needles by flaming them in a Bunsen burner until red-hot.
2. Open culture tubes or plates carefully to minimize exposure to airborne contaminants.
3. Transfer microbial cultures using sterile loops or pipettes.
4. Flame the neck of culture tubes before and after transfer to prevent contamination.

5. Work near a flame or inside a laminar airflow cabinet for added sterility.

Results:

Successful aseptic transfer will result in pure cultures without contamination.

Discussion Questions and Answers:

1. **Why is flaming the inoculating loop important?**
   - o It ensures sterility by killing any residual microorganisms.
2. **What precautions should be taken while working in a laminar airflow cabinet?**
   - o Avoid unnecessary movements and work with sterile materials only.
3. **Why should culture tubes be flamed before and after use?**
   - o To prevent airborne contaminants from entering the tubes.

Experiment 39: Preparation of Media to Culture Microorganisms

Aim: To prepare different types of media for the cultivation of microorganisms.

Principle: Microbial culture media provide essential nutrients and conditions required for the growth of microorganisms. Media can be classified into liquid (broth) or solid (agar) based on their physical state and can be complex or synthetic based on composition.

Preparation of Reagents:

1. **Nutrient Broth:**
   a) Peptone - 5 g
   b) Beef extract - 3 g
   c) Sodium chloride - 5 g
   d) Distilled water - up to 1 L

2. **Nutrient Agar:**
   a) Nutrient broth components + Agar - 15 g

3. **MacConkey Agar:**
   a) Peptone - 20 g
   b) Lactose - 10 g
   c) Bile salts - 5 g
   d) Neutral red - 0.075 g
   e) Agar - 15 g
   f) Distilled water - up to 1 L

4. **Sabouraud Dextrose Agar (SDA):**

a) Peptone - 10 g

b) Dextrose - 40 g

c) Agar - 15 g

d) Distilled water - up to 1 L

Procedure:

1. Weigh the required quantity of media components.

2. Dissolve the components in distilled water by stirring.

3. Adjust the pH of the media to the required level (e.g., pH 7.0 for nutrient broth).

4. Autoclave the prepared media at 121°C for 15 minutes at 15 psi.

5. Pour the sterilized media into petri dishes or test tubes under aseptic conditions.

6. Allow the media to solidify (for solid media) before use.

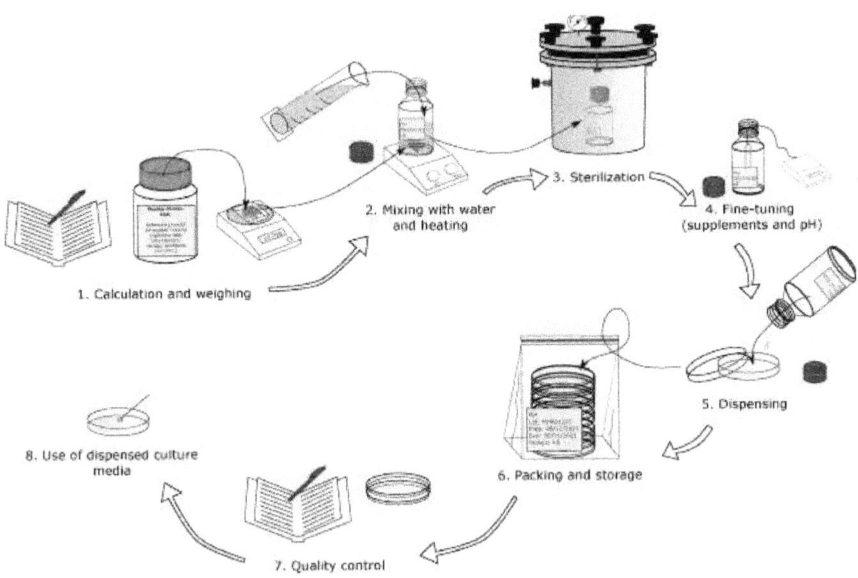

Results:

Prepared media should appear clear without contamination and ready for microbial inoculation.

Discussion Questions and Answers:

1. **Why is autoclaving important in media preparation?**
   - It ensures sterility by killing all microbial contaminants.

2. **What is the purpose of adding agar to media?**
   - It provides a solid surface for microbial growth.

3. **Why is pH adjustment important in media preparation?**
   - Microorganisms require an optimal pH for growth and metabolic activity.

4. **What are the differences between selective and differential media?**
   - Selective media inhibit the growth of unwanted organisms, while differential media differentiate microorganisms based on metabolic properties

Experiment 40: Dilution Techniques and Pipetting

Aim: To perform accurate dilution techniques and pipetting for microbiological and biochemical applications.

Principle: Dilution techniques are used to reduce the concentration of solutions to desired levels, ensuring proper experimental conditions. Proper pipetting ensures accurate measurement and transfer of liquids, which is crucial for experimental reproducibility.

Preparation of Reagents:

1. **Stock Solution:**
   a) Prepare a concentrated stock solution of a known substance (e.g., glucose, NaCl).

2. **Dilution Buffer:**
   a) Sterile distilled water or appropriate buffer (e.g., phosphate-buffered saline).

Procedure:

Serial Dilution Method:

1. Take 9 mL of dilution buffer into sterile test tubes.
2. Add 1 mL of stock solution into the first test tube (10^{-1} dilution).
3. Mix well and transfer 1 mL from the first test tube to the next tube (10^{-2} dilution).
4. Repeat the process to obtain required dilutions.
5. Plate appropriate dilutions to analyze microbial count.

Pipetting Technique:

1. Select the appropriate pipette and set the desired volume.

2. Pre-wet the pipette tip by aspirating and dispensing the liquid once.

3. Immerse the tip into the sample and slowly aspirate the required volume.

4. Dispense the liquid carefully by pressing the plunger to the first stop.

5. Eject the tip into a waste container after use.

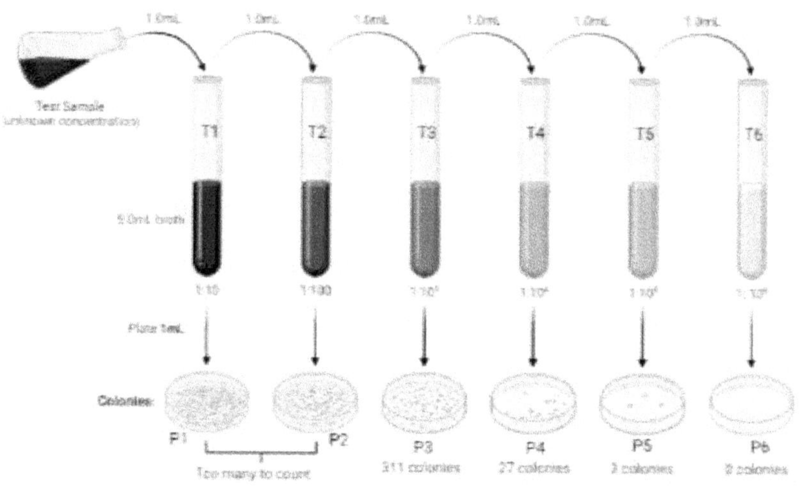

Results:

Accurate dilutions and pipetting result in precise and reproducible experimental outcomes.

Discussion Questions and Answers:

1. **Why are serial dilutions used in microbiological analysis?**
   - To reduce microbial concentrations to countable levels.
2. **What is the significance of proper pipetting technique?**
   - It ensures accuracy and consistency in experiments.
3. **Why should the pipette tip be pre-wetted before use?**
   - To ensure consistent sample delivery by minimizing evaporation and adherence.
4. **How can errors be minimized during dilution techniques?**
   - By using calibrated pipettes and mixing solutions thoroughly.

Experiment 41: Microbes Culture in Broth and Solid Media, Colony Characteristics, and Counting of Colonies (Serial Dilution Method)

Aim: To culture microorganisms in broth and solid media, study their colony characteristics, and count colonies using the serial dilution method.

Principle:

Microbial culture involves growing microorganisms in nutrient-rich media under controlled conditions. Broth culture supports uniform growth, while solid media allow for colony formation. The serial dilution method helps to quantify microbial populations by progressively diluting the sample and plating it onto solid media.

Preparation of Reagents:

1. **Nutrient Broth:**
   a) Peptone - 5 g
   b) Beef extract - 3 g
   c) Sodium chloride - 5 g
   d) Distilled water - up to 1 L

2. **Nutrient Agar:**
   a) Nutrient broth components + Agar - 15 g

3. **Serial Dilution Buffer:**
   a) Sterile physiological saline (0.85% NaCl)

Procedure:

Microbial Culture in Broth:

1. Prepare nutrient broth and sterilize by autoclaving.
2. Inoculate the broth with microbial culture under aseptic conditions.
3. Incubate at 37°C for 24-48 hours.
4. Observe turbidity indicating microbial growth.

Microbial Culture on Solid Media:

1. Prepare nutrient agar and pour into sterile petri dishes.
2. Allow the agar to solidify and inoculate using streak or spread plate techniques.
3. Incubate at 37°C for 24-48 hours.
4. Observe colony characteristics (size, shape, color, texture).

Serial Dilution and Colony Counting:

1. Prepare a series of tenfold dilutions of the microbial sample.
2. Plate 0.1 mL of each dilution onto nutrient agar plates.
3. Incubate the plates at 37°C for 24 hours.
4. Count the colonies and calculate colony-forming units (CFU) using the formula:

Results:

The number of colonies counted corresponds to the microbial load in the original sample.

Discussion Questions and Answers:

1. **Why is serial dilution used in microbial counting?**
   - It helps in reducing microbial concentration to countable levels.
2. **What are the key colony characteristics observed on solid media?**
   - Size, shape, color, elevation, margin, and texture.
3. **Why is aseptic technique important in microbial culture?**
   - To prevent contamination and ensure accurate results.
4. **What is the significance of turbidity in broth culture?**
   - It indicates microbial growth in liquid media.

Experiment 42: Bacterial Colony Morphology

Aim: To observe and describe the morphological characteristics of bacterial colonies.

Principle: Bacterial colonies exhibit unique characteristics on solid media, which can be used to identify and differentiate bacterial species based on their appearance.

Procedure:

1. Streak a bacterial culture on a nutrient agar plate.
2. Incubate the plate at 37°C for 24-48 hours.
3. Observe and record the colony morphology based on the following criteria:
   - Size (small, medium, large)
   - Shape (circular, irregular, rhizoid)
   - Margin (entire, undulate, lobate)
   - Elevation (flat, convex, raised)
   - Surface texture (smooth, rough, wrinkled)
   - Opacity (transparent, translucent, opaque)
   - Color (pigmented, non-pigmented)

Results:

Colony Morphology of Bacteria

MARGIN	COLOUR	ELEVATION	TEXTURE	SHAPE
Curled	Orange	Raised	Slimy, moist	Round
Entire (smooth)	Red or pink	Umbonate	Matte, brittle	Punctiform
Filamentous	Black	Flat	Shiny, viscous	Rhizoid (root-like)
Undulate (wavy)	Brown	Convex	Dry, mucoid	Filamentous
Lobate	Opaque or white	Pulvinate (Cushion-shaped)	Translucent	Irregular
Erose (serrated)	Milky	Growth into culture medium	Iridescent (changes colour in reflected light)	Spindle

Bacterial colonies will be categorized based on their observed morphological characteristics.

Discussion Questions and Answers:

1. **Why is bacterial colony morphology important?**
   - It helps in the preliminary identification and differentiation of bacteria.

2. **What factors can influence colony morphology?**

   o   Nutrient availability, incubation temperature, and agar composition.

3. **What does an opaque colony indicate?**

   o   It suggests dense growth with significant biomass production.

Experiment 43: Quantitative Determination of Bacterial Populations

Aim: To quantify bacterial populations using the serial dilution and plate count method.

Principle: The quantitative determination of bacterial populations involves serial dilution of a sample followed by plating on a suitable agar medium. Colony-forming units (CFUs) are counted, and the bacterial concentration is calculated based on the dilution factor.

Preparation of Reagents:

1. **Sterile Saline Solution (0.85% NaCl):**
    a) Sodium chloride - 8.5 g
    b) Distilled water - up to 1 L

2. **Nutrient Agar:**
    a) Peptone - 5 g
    b) Beef extract - 3 g
    c) Agar - 15 g
    d) Distilled water - up to 1 L

Procedure:

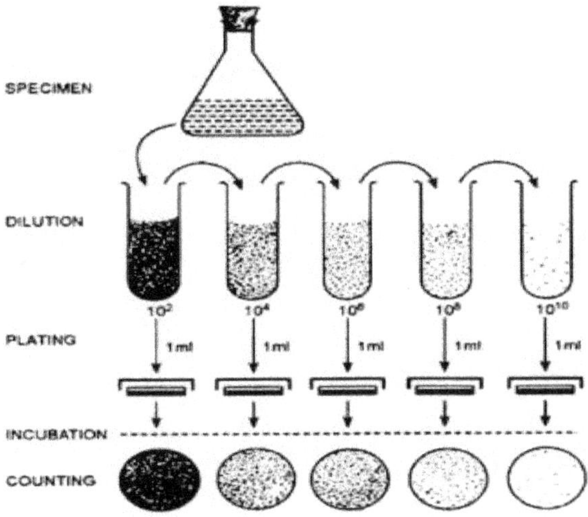

1. Prepare serial dilutions by transferring 1 mL of the bacterial sample into 9 mL of sterile saline solution (10^{-1} dilution).

2. Continue the serial dilution up to the desired dilution factor (e.g., 10^{-6}).

3. Pipette 0.1 mL of each dilution onto sterile nutrient agar plates.

4. Spread the inoculum evenly using a sterile spreader.

5. Incubate the plates at 37°C for 24-48 hours.

6. Count the colonies on plates with 30-300 colonies.

7. Calculate the bacterial population using the formula:

Results:

The bacterial concentration is expressed as CFU/mL of the original sample.

Discussion Questions and Answers:

1. **Why are serial dilutions necessary in bacterial enumeration?**
   - To reduce the bacterial count to a countable range.
2. **What is the ideal colony range for accurate counting?**
   - 30-300 colonies per plate.
3. **What factors can influence colony count accuracy?**
   - Incubation time, temperature, and even distribution of sample on the plate.
4. **Why is it important to report results as CFU/mL rather than individual cells?**
   - Because CFU accounts for clusters and chains of bacteria rather than single cells.

Experiment 44: Gram Staining

Aim: To differentiate bacterial species based on their cell wall composition using the Gram staining technique.

Principle: Gram staining differentiates bacteria into Gram-positive and Gram-negative based on the thickness of their peptidoglycan layer. Gram-positive bacteria retain the crystal violet stain, appearing purple, whereas Gram-negative bacteria lose the stain and take up the counterstain, appearing pink.

Procedure:

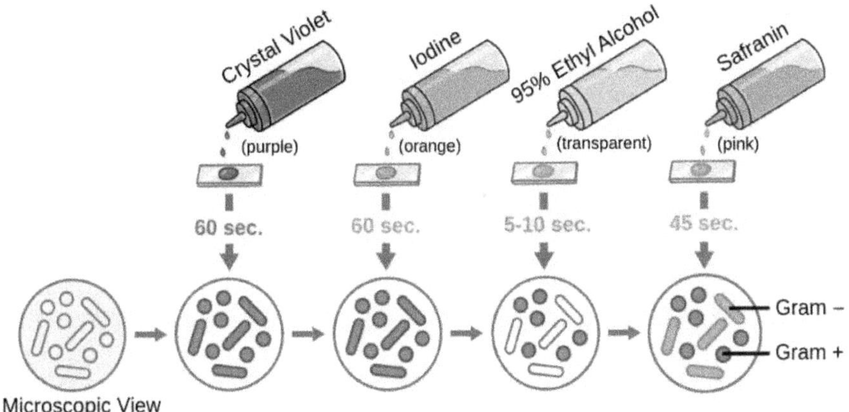

1. Prepare a bacterial smear on a glass slide and heat-fix it.
2. Flood the slide with crystal violet for 1 minute and rinse with water.
3. Apply iodine solution for 1 minute and rinse with water.
4. Decolorize with alcohol for 15-20 seconds and rinse immediately.

5. Counterstain with safranin for 1 minute and rinse with water.

6. Air-dry and observe under a microscope using oil immersion.

Results:

- Gram-positive bacteria: Purple color
- Gram-negative bacteria: Pink color

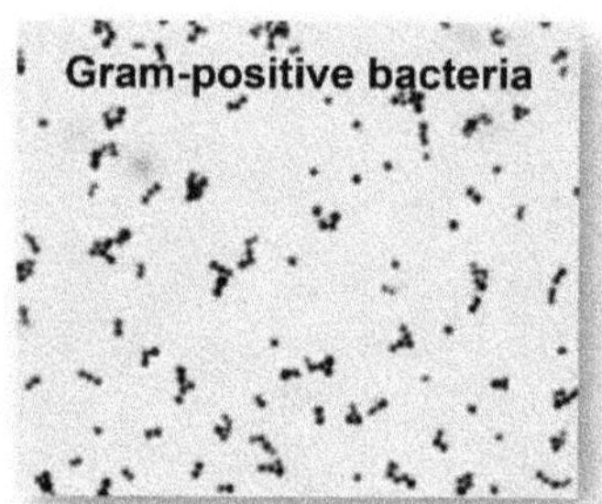

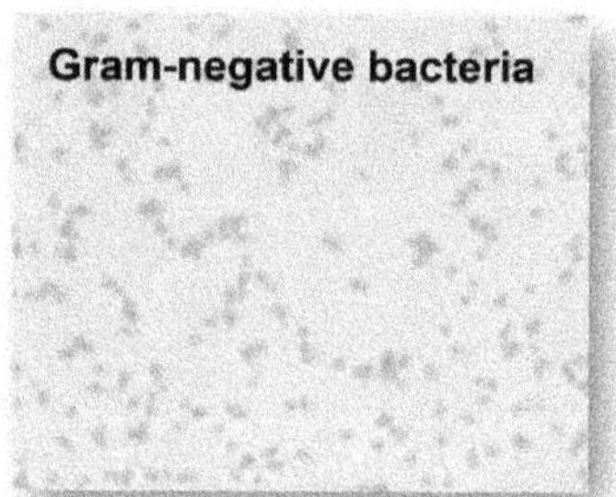

Discussion Questions and Answers:

1. **Why is heat fixation necessary before staining?**
   - It helps adhere bacteria to the slide and kills the cells.
2. **What is the role of iodine in Gram staining?**
   - It acts as a mordant to fix the crystal violet stain.
3. **Why do Gram-negative bacteria appear pink?**
   - Their thin peptidoglycan layer does not retain the crystal violet stain after decolorization.

Experiment 45: Biochemical Tests for the identification and characterization of bacterial species.

Aim: To perform various biochemical tests for the identification and characterization of bacterial species.

Principle: Biochemical tests are used to detect enzymatic activities and metabolic pathways in bacteria, helping in their identification based on physiological characteristics.

Procedure:

Test Name	Principle	Procedure	Observation
Indole Test	Detects the presence of tryptophanase, which breaks down tryptophan to produce indole.	Inoculate bacteria in tryptone broth, incubate, and add Kovac's reagent.	Red ring formation indicates positive test.
Methyl Red Test	Determines acid production from glucose fermentation.	Inoculate bacteria in MR-VP broth, incubate, and add methyl red indicator.	Red color indicates positive test.
Voges-Proskauer Test	Detects acetoin production from glucose fermentation.	Inoculate in MR-VP broth, incubate, and add Barritt's reagents A & B.	Red color development indicates positive test.

Citrate Utilization Test	Determines the ability of bacteria to use citrate as the sole carbon source.	Streak bacteria on Simmons' citrate agar and incubate.	Blue color indicates positive test.
Triple Sugar Iron (TSI) Test	Differentiates bacteria based on sugar fermentation and hydrogen sulfide production.	Stab and streak bacteria on TSI agar slant and incubate.	Yellow slant/butt (fermentation), black precipitate (H_2S).
Starch Hydrolysis Test	Determines the ability to hydrolyze starch using amylase.	Streak bacteria on starch agar, incubate, and add iodine solution.	Clear zone around growth indicates positive test.
Gelatin Hydrolysis Test	Detects gelatinase activity to hydrolyze gelatin.	Inoculate gelatin tube, incubate, and refrigerate.	Liquefaction of gelatin indicates positive test.
Catalase Test	Detects the presence of catalase enzyme, which breaks down hydrogen peroxide.	Add hydrogen peroxide to bacterial colony.	Bubbling indicates positive test.
Oxidase Test	Identifies bacteria producing cytochrome oxidase enzyme.	Place bacteria on oxidase strip or reagent drop.	Purple color indicates positive test.

Results:

Bacteria are characterized based on their biochemical reactions.

Discussion Questions and Answers:

1. **Why is the Voges-Proskauer test performed?**
   - To detect the production of acetoin, an intermediate in glucose fermentation.
2. **What does a positive citrate utilization test indicate?**
   - It indicates the ability of bacteria to use citrate as the sole carbon source.
3. **Why is the catalase test important?**
   - It helps differentiate bacteria based on their ability to break down hydrogen peroxide.

Experiment 46: Staining Techniques

Aim: To observe bacterial cell morphology and structures using various staining techniques.

Principle: Staining techniques are used to enhance contrast in microscopic observations, allowing for the differentiation of bacterial cells and structures based on their physical and chemical properties.

Preparation of Reagents:

1. **Crystal Violet Solution (Gram Staining):**
   a) Crystal violet - 2 g
   b) Ethanol (95%) - 20 mL
   c) Distilled water - up to 100 mL

2. **Iodine Solution (Gram Staining):**
   a) Iodine - 1 g
   b) Potassium iodide - 2 g
   c) Distilled water - up to 100 mL

3. **Safranin Solution (Gram Staining):**
   a) Safranin - 2.5 g
   b) Ethanol (95%) - 10 mL
   c) Distilled water - up to 100 mL

4. **Carbol Fuchsin Solution (Acid-Fast Staining):**
   a) Basic fuchsin - 1 g
   b) Phenol - 5 g
   c) Distilled water - up to 100 mL

5. **Acid-Alcohol (Decolorizer for Acid-Fast Staining):**

   a) Hydrochloric acid - 3 mL

   b) Ethanol (95%) - 97 mL

6. **Malachite Green Solution (Endospore Staining):**

   a) Malachite green - 5 g

   b) Distilled water - up to 100 mL

7. **Nigrosin Solution (Negative Staining):**

   a) Nigrosin - 1 g

   b) Distilled water - up to 100 mL

8. **India Ink Solution (Capsule Staining):**

   a) India ink - 5 mL

   b) Distilled water - up to 100 mL

Procedure:

Staining Technique	Principle	Procedure	Observation
Simple Staining	Uses a single dye to visualize cell morphology.	Stain the heat-fixed smear with methylene blue for 1 minute, rinse, and observe under the microscope.	Cells appear uniformly stained.
Gram Staining	Differentiates bacteria based on cell wall composition.	Stain with crystal violet, apply iodine, decolorize with alcohol, and	Gram-positive (purple), Gram-negative (pink).

		counterstain with safranin.	
Endospore Staining	Detects bacterial endospores.	Stain with malachite green, heat, rinse, and counterstain with safranin.	Endospores appear green, vegetative cells red.
Capsule Staining	Identifies bacterial capsules.	Stain with India ink or crystal violet, observe under the microscope without heat fixing.	Capsules appear as clear halos around cells.
Acid-Fast (AFB) Staining	Identifies mycobacteria based on mycolic acid content.	Stain with carbol fuchsin, decolorize with acid alcohol, counterstain with methylene blue.	Acid-fast bacteria (red), non-acid-fast (blue).
Negative Staining	Provides contrast by staining the background rather than the cells.	Mix bacteria with nigrosin or India ink and observe under the microscope.	Cells appear clear against a dark background.

Results:

Bacterial cells and structures are visualized based on their staining properties.

Discussion Questions and Answers:

1. **Why is Gram staining important in bacterial classification?**
   - o It helps in differentiating bacteria based on cell wall composition, aiding in identification and treatment decisions.

2. **What does a positive acid-fast stain indicate?**
   - o The presence of mycobacteria with waxy cell walls resistant to decolorization.

3. **Why is heat used in endospore staining?**
   - o Heat helps in the penetration of malachite green into the tough endospore coat.

4. **What is the purpose of negative staining?**
   - o It allows observation of cell morphology without distortion due to heat fixing.

Experiment 47: Microbial Examination of Food and Detection of Pathogenic Bacteria from Food Samples

Aim: To detect and quantify pathogenic bacteria in food samples using microbiological techniques.

Principle: Foodborne pathogens can cause serious health issues and must be detected to ensure food safety. Common techniques such as serial dilution, plating, and selective media help isolate and identify specific bacteria.

Preparation of Reagents:

1. **Nutrient Agar:**
   a) Peptone - 5 g
   b) Beef extract - 3 g
   c) Agar - 15 g
   d) Distilled water - up to 1 L

2. **MacConkey Agar:**
   a) Peptone - 20 g
   b) Lactose - 10 g
   c) Bile salts - 5 g
   d) Neutral red - 0.075 g
   e) Agar - 15 g
   f) Distilled water - up to 1 L

3. **XLD Agar:**
   a) Yeast extract - 3 g
   b) Xylose - 3.75 g

c) Lysine - 5 g

d) Sodium thiosulfate - 6.8 g

e) Agar - 15 g

f) Distilled water - up to 1 L

4. **Saline Solution:**

a) Sodium chloride - 8.5 g

b) Distilled water - up to 1 L

Procedure:

1. **Sample Preparation:**
   - Homogenize food sample in sterile peptone water.
   - Perform serial dilutions to reduce bacterial concentration.

2. **Plating Methods:**
   - Spread 0.1 mL of diluted sample onto selective and differential media such as:
     - MacConkey agar (for coliforms)
     - XLD agar (for Salmonella)
     - Mannitol salt agar (for Staphylococcus aureus)

3. **Incubation:**
   - Incubate plates at 37°C for 24-48 hours.

4. **Colony Counting:**
   - Count distinct colonies and calculate CFU/mL using:

5. **Biochemical Identification:**

o   Perform biochemical tests such as Indole, Methyl Red, Voges-Proskauer, and Citrate tests to confirm bacterial identity.

Results:

Presence of distinct colony morphology on selective media confirms the presence of specific bacteria.

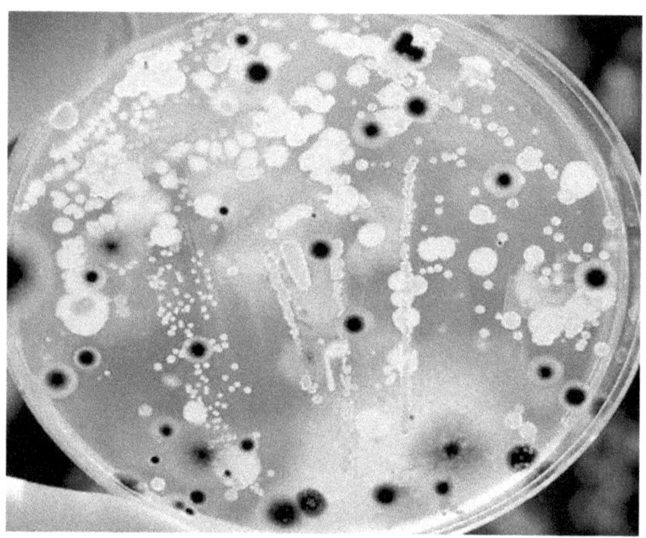

Discussion Questions and Answers:

1. **Why is serial dilution necessary in food microbiology?**
   - o It reduces the microbial load to countable levels for accurate enumeration.
2. **Which bacteria are commonly detected in food samples?**
   - o Pathogens such as E. coli, Salmonella, and Staphylococcus aureus.

3. **What is the significance of using selective media?**

   o   It helps isolate and identify specific bacteria by inhibiting unwanted microbial growth.

4. **Why is food microbiological examination important?**

   o   To ensure food safety and prevent foodborne illnesses.

Experiment 48: Microbial Fermentations for the Production and Estimation of Ethanol

Aim: To produce and estimate ethanol qualitatively and quantitatively through microbial fermentation.

Principle: Microorganisms such as Saccharomyces cerevisiae ferment sugars under anaerobic conditions, producing ethanol and carbon dioxide. The ethanol concentration can be estimated using qualitative and quantitative methods such as the iodine test and spectrophotometry.

Preparation of Reagents:

1. **Fermentation Medium:**
   a) Glucose - 100 g
   b) Yeast extract - 10 g
   c) Peptone - 5 g
   d) Distilled water - up to 1 L
   e) Adjust pH to 5.0

2. **Iodine Solution (Qualitative Test):**
   a) Iodine crystals - 1 g
   b) Potassium iodide - 2 g
   c) Distilled water - up to 100 mL

3. **Distillation Setup (Quantitative Estimation):**
   a) Distilled water
   b) 5% Sulfuric acid

4. **Standard Ethanol Solution:** Prepare a range of known ethanol concentrations for calibration.

Procedure:

Production of Ethanol:

1. Prepare a fermentation medium containing glucose, yeast extract, and necessary salts.
2. Inoculate with Saccharomyces cerevisiae and incubate at 30°C for 48-72 hours under anaerobic conditions.
3. Collect the fermented broth for analysis.

Qualitative Estimation (Iodine Test):

1. Take 2 mL of fermented broth in a test tube.
2. Add a few drops of iodine solution.
3. Observe the color change indicating the presence of ethanol.

Quantitative Estimation (Spectrophotometry):

1. Distill the fermented broth to concentrate ethanol.
2. Measure absorbance at 600 nm using a spectrophotometer.
3. Compare with a standard ethanol curve to determine concentration.

Results:

Ethanol production is confirmed by qualitative color change and quantitatively measured using spectrophotometry.

Discussion Questions and Answers:

1. **Why is *Saccharomyces cerevisiae* commonly used in ethanol production?**
   - It efficiently ferments sugars to ethanol under anaerobic conditions.

2. **What factors influence ethanol production in fermentation?**
   - Temperature, pH, sugar concentration, and incubation time.

3. **Why is spectrophotometry used for ethanol estimation?**
   - It provides a rapid and accurate quantification of ethanol concentration

Experiment 49: Isolation of Air Microflora

Aim: To isolate and identify microorganisms present in the air using different sampling techniques.

Principle: Airborne microorganisms can be isolated using passive and active sampling methods. The exposure plate method allows microbes to settle onto nutrient-rich media by gravity, while the rotorod sampler method actively collects airborne particles onto a sampling surface.

Procedure:

(a) Exposure Plate Method:

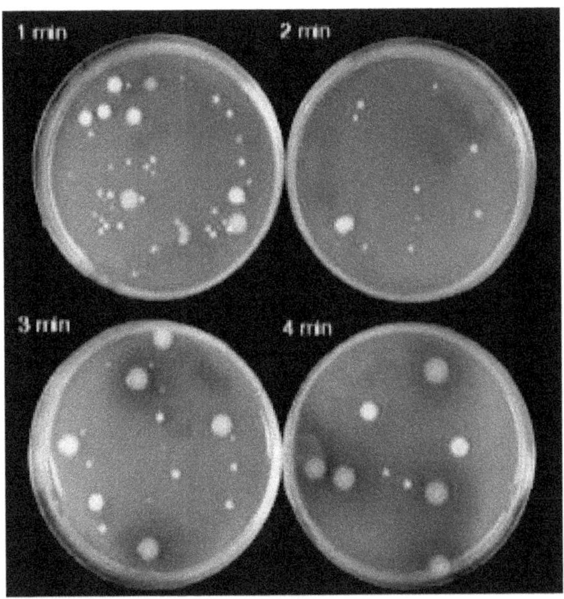

1. Prepare sterile nutrient agar plates.

2. Expose the plates to the air at different locations for 30-60 minutes.

3. Cover the plates and incubate them at 37°C for 24-48 hours.

4. Observe and count the colonies formed on the plates.

(b) Rotorod Sampler Method:

1. Set up the rotorod sampler with sterile sampling rods.

2. Run the sampler at the desired airflow rate for a specified period.

3. Transfer the collected particles onto nutrient agar plates.

4. Incubate the plates at 37°C for 24-48 hours.

5. Count and identify the microbial colonies.

Results:

The number and types of colonies observed indicate the microbial load and diversity in the air sample.

Discussion Questions and Answers:

1. **Why is the exposure plate method used for air sampling?**

   ➢ It provides a simple and cost-effective means of assessing airborne contamination.

2. **What are the advantages of the rotorod sampler method over the exposure plate method?**

   ➢ It allows quantitative sampling with better precision and efficiency in detecting airborne microorganisms.

3. **What factors influence microbial presence in the air?**

   ➢ Environmental factors such as temperature, humidity, and airflow.

Experiment 50: Testing of Water Quality (Coliform Test), H₂S Strip Method

Aim: To assess the microbial quality of water by detecting coliform bacteria using the coliform test and H_2S strip method.

Principle: Coliform bacteria are indicators of fecal contamination in water. The coliform test and H_2S strip method detect the presence of these bacteria based on their ability to ferment lactose and produce hydrogen sulfide gas.

Procedure:

Coliform Test:

1. Collect water samples in sterile bottles.
2. Inoculate lactose broth with the water sample.
3. Incubate at 37°C for 24-48 hours.
4. Observe for gas production in Durham tubes, indicating coliform presence.

H₂S Strip Method:

1. Immerse an H_2S strip into the water sample in a sterile bottle.
2. Incubate at room temperature for 24-48 hours.
3. Observe the strip for blackening, indicating the presence of hydrogen sulfide-producing bacteria.

Results:

- Positive coliform test: Gas production in Durham tubes.

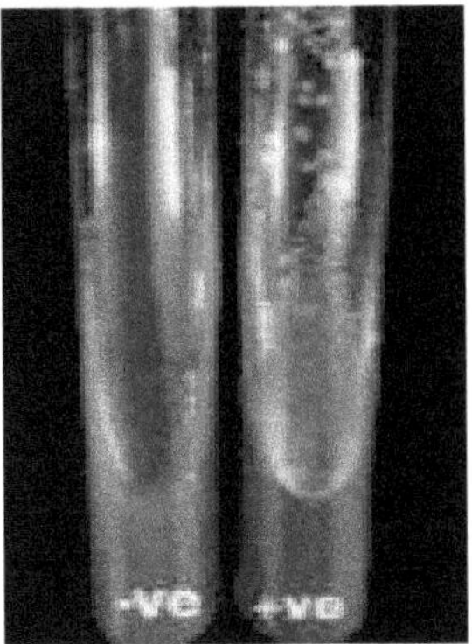

- Positive H₂S test: Black precipitate formation on the strip.

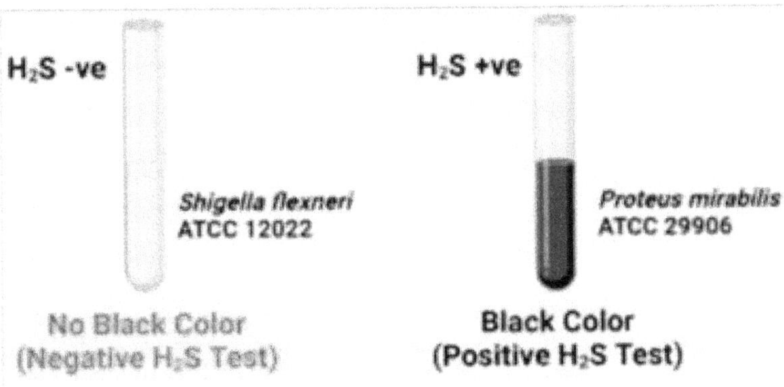

-

Discussion Questions and Answers:

1. **Why is the coliform test used for water quality assessment?**
   - It detects fecal contamination, ensuring water safety for consumption.

2. **What does a positive H₂S strip test indicate?**

- o Presence of hydrogen sulfide-producing bacteria, which suggests possible contamination.

3. **Why is lactose broth used in the coliform test?**

- o It provides a nutrient-rich medium for coliform bacteria to ferment lactose and produce gas.

4. **How can water contamination be prevented?**

- o By proper treatment methods such as filtration, chlorination, and boiling

Experiment 51: Preparation of Murashige and Skoog (MS) Media

Aim: To prepare Murashige and Skoog (MS) medium for plant tissue culture.

Principle: MS medium is a widely used plant tissue culture medium that provides essential macro and micronutrients, vitamins, and growth regulators to support plant cell growth and development.

Preparation of Reagents:

1. **Macronutrients Solution:**

    a) NH_4NO_3 - 1650 mg

    b) KNO_3 - 1900 mg

    c) $CaCl_2 \cdot 2H_2O$ - 440 mg

    d) $MgSO_4 \cdot 7H_2O$ - 370 mg

    e) KH_2PO_4 - 170 mg

2. **Micronutrients Solution:**

    a) H_3BO_3 - 6.2 mg

    b) $MnSO_4 \cdot H_2O$ - 16.9 mg

    c) $ZnSO_4 \cdot 7H_2O$ - 8.6 mg

    d) $Na_2MoO_4 \cdot 2H_2O$ - 0.25 mg

    e) $CuSO_4 \cdot 5H_2O$ - 0.025 mg

    f) $CoCl_2 \cdot 6H_2O$ - 0.025 mg

3. **Vitamins Solution:**

   a) Myo-inositol - 100 mg

   b) Thiamine HCl - 0.1 mg

   c) Pyridoxine HCl - 0.5 mg

   d) Nicotinic acid - 0.5 mg

4. **Sucrose:** 30 g
5. **Agar (for solid medium):** 8 g
6. **pH Adjustment:** Adjust the pH to 5.7 using NaOH or HCl.

Procedure:

1. Dissolve macronutrients, micronutrients, and vitamins in distilled water.
2. Add sucrose and dissolve completely.
3. Adjust pH to 5.7.
4. Add agar if preparing solid media.
5. Autoclave at 121°C for 15 minutes.
6. Dispense into sterile culture vessels under aseptic conditions.

Discussion Questions and Answers:

1. **What is the significance of Murashige and Skoog (MS) medium in plant tissue culture?**

    o It provides essential nutrients required for plant cell growth and differentiation.

2. **Why is sucrose added to MS media?**

    o Sucrose acts as a carbon source for the growth of plant tissues.

3. **What is the purpose of adjusting the pH of the MS medium?**

    o pH affects nutrient availability and optimal growth of plant tissues.

4. **Why is agar used in the preparation of solid MS media?**

    o Agar solidifies the medium, providing support for plant explants.

5. **How is sterilization of MS media achieved?**

- The media is autoclaved at 121°C for 15 minutes to ensure sterility.

Experiment 52: Sterilization Techniques and Inoculation of Various Explants

Aim: To study different sterilization techniques and perform inoculation of various plant explants in a sterile environment.

Principle: Sterilization is essential in plant tissue culture to eliminate microbial contaminants. Various sterilization techniques such as chemical, heat, and radiation sterilization are used to ensure aseptic conditions before inoculating explants.

Preparation of Reagents:

1. **Sterilization Solutions:**

    a) Sodium hypochlorite (2-5%)

    b) Ethanol (70%)

    c) Mercuric chloride (0.1%)

    d) Distilled sterile water

2. **Murashige and Skoog (MS) Medium:**

    a) Prepared and autoclaved as per standard protocol.

Procedure:

1. **Surface Sterilization of Explants:**
    o Wash explants with running tap water for 15 minutes.
    o Dip in 70% ethanol for 30 seconds.

- o Immerse in sodium hypochlorite solution for 5-10 minutes with occasional shaking.
- o Rinse thoroughly with sterile distilled water 3-4 times.

2. **Inoculation of Explants:** Under aseptic conditions in a laminar airflow hood, transfer the sterilized explants onto the prepared MS medium. Seal the culture vessels and label appropriately.

3. Place the inoculated cultures in a growth chamber under controlled light and temperature conditions.

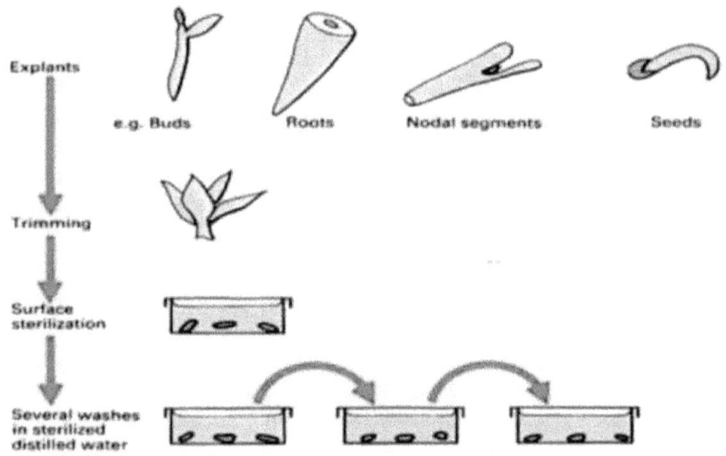

Results:

Successful inoculation is indicated by contamination-free growth of explants.

Discussion Questions and Answers:

1. **Why is sterilization important in plant tissue culture?**
   - To prevent microbial contamination that can hinder plant growth.
2. **What are the commonly used sterilization agents for explants?**
   - Sodium hypochlorite, ethanol, and mercuric chloride.
3. **Why is ethanol used for sterilization?**
   - Ethanol acts as a disinfectant by denaturing proteins and dissolving lipids.
4. **What is the role of a laminar airflow hood in inoculation?**
   - It provides a sterile environment for handling plant tissues.
5. **How can contamination in culture be identified?**
   - By observing fungal or bacterial growth in the culture medium.

Experiment 53: Aseptic Manipulation of Various Explants

Aim: To perform aseptic manipulation of various plant explants for tissue culture.

Principle: Aseptic manipulation ensures that plant explants remain free from microbial contamination during handling and culture establishment. Proper sterilization and handling techniques prevent contamination and promote healthy plant growth.

Procedure:

1. Prepare work area by disinfecting with 70% ethanol.
2. Sterilize forceps, scalpels, and other tools by autoclaving or flame sterilization.
3. Select healthy plant explants and perform surface sterilization.
4. Transfer explants to sterile petri dishes or culture vessels under laminar airflow.
5. Carefully inoculate explants onto growth media using sterile forceps.
6. Seal the culture vessels and incubate under controlled conditions.

Results:

Successful aseptic manipulation results in uncontaminated, healthy explant growth.

Discussion Questions and Answers:

1. **Why is aseptic manipulation crucial in tissue culture?**
   - To avoid contamination and ensure healthy plant development.
2. **What precautions should be taken during aseptic handling?**
   - Use of sterile tools, working in a laminar airflow hood, and maintaining personal hygiene.
3. **How can aseptic conditions be maintained during culture transfer?**
   - By working quickly, using sterile equipment, and avoiding unnecessary exposure to the environment.

Experiment 54: Callus Induction and Plant Regeneration

Aim: To induce callus formation from plant explants and achieve plant regeneration under in vitro conditions.

Principle: Callus formation and plant regeneration in tissue culture depend on the balance of plant growth regulators such as auxins and cytokinins. Callus is an unorganized mass of cells that can be induced from plant explants by exposing them to a suitable nutrient medium with specific hormonal concentrations.

Preparation of Reagents:

1. **Murashige and Skoog (MS) Medium:**

a) Macronutrients and micronutrients as per standard formulation.

b) Vitamins and sucrose (30 g/L).

c) Agar (8 g/L) for solid medium.

d) pH adjusted to 5.7.

2. **Growth Regulators:**

a) 2,4-D (2,4-Dichlorophenoxyacetic acid) - for callus induction.

b) BAP (6-Benzylaminopurine) - for shoot induction.

c) NAA (Naphthaleneacetic acid) - for root induction.

Procedure:

1. **Callus Induction:**
   - Select healthy explants such as leaf, stem, or root sections.
   - Sterilize explants using ethanol (70%) and sodium hypochlorite (2-5%).
   - Place the explants onto MS medium supplemented with 2,4-D (1-2 mg/L).
   - Incubate under dark conditions at 25°C for 2-3 weeks.
   - Observe callus formation.

2. **Plant Regeneration:**

- o Transfer callus to regeneration medium containing BAP and NAA.
- o Maintain under 16 hours light and 8 hours dark photoperiod.
- o Monitor shoot and root development.

3. **Hardening and Acclimatization:**
   - o Transfer regenerated plants to pots with soil mixture.
   - o Gradually acclimatize plants to environmental conditions by exposing them to natural light and humidity.
   - o Water regularly and monitor growth.

Successful callus induction and subsequent regeneration of shoots and roots will be observed.

Discussion Questions and Answers:

1. **What is the role of auxins and cytokinins in callus induction and plant regeneration?**
   - Auxins promote callus formation, while cytokinins help in shoot regeneration.

2. **Why is MS medium commonly used in plant tissue culture?**
   - It provides all essential nutrients required for plant growth and development.

3. **What factors influence callus induction?**
   - Type of explant, hormonal concentration, and environmental conditions.

4. **Why is the hardening process important after plant regeneration?**
   - It helps the regenerated plants adapt to external environmental conditions.

5. **What are the applications of callus culture in biotechnology?**
   - Used for genetic transformation, secondary metabolite production, and conservation of plant species.

Experiment 55: Anther, Embryo, and Endosperm Culture

Aim: To study the in vitro culture of anther, embryo, and endosperm for plant regeneration.

Principle: Anther, embryo, and endosperm culture are advanced tissue culture techniques used for haploid production, somatic embryogenesis, and triploid plant development, respectively. These methods facilitate plant breeding, genetic improvement, and conservation.

Preparation of Reagents:

1. **Murashige and Skoog (MS) Medium:**

   a) Macronutrients and micronutrients as per standard formulation.
   b) Vitamins and sucrose (30 g/L).
   c) Agar (8 g/L) for solid medium.
   d) pH adjusted to 5.7.

2. **Growth Regulators:**

   a) BAP (6-Benzylaminopurine) - for shoot induction.
   b) NAA (Naphthaleneacetic acid) - for root induction.
   c) 2,4-D (Dichlorophenoxyacetic acid) - for callus formation.

Procedure:

1. Anther Culture:

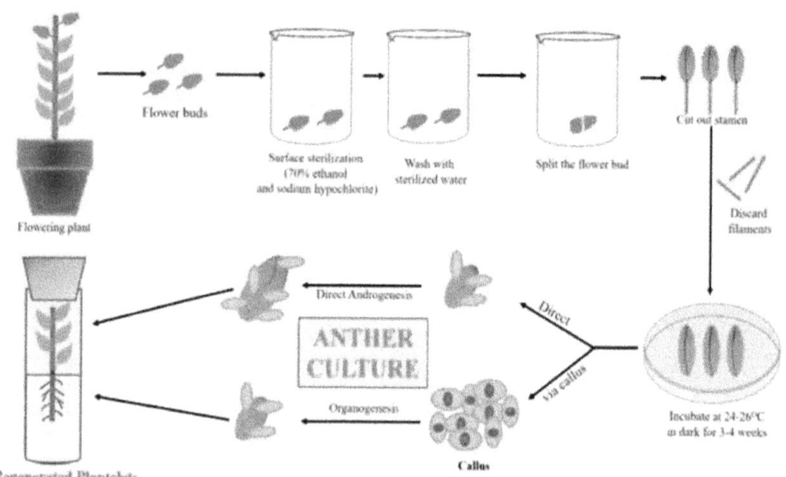

- Collect flower buds at the appropriate developmental stage.
- Surface sterilize with ethanol (70%) and sodium hypochlorite (2-5%).
- Excise anthers and place them on MS medium containing BAP and NAA.
- Incubate under controlled conditions and observe for callus formation and shoot initiation.

2. Embryo Culture:

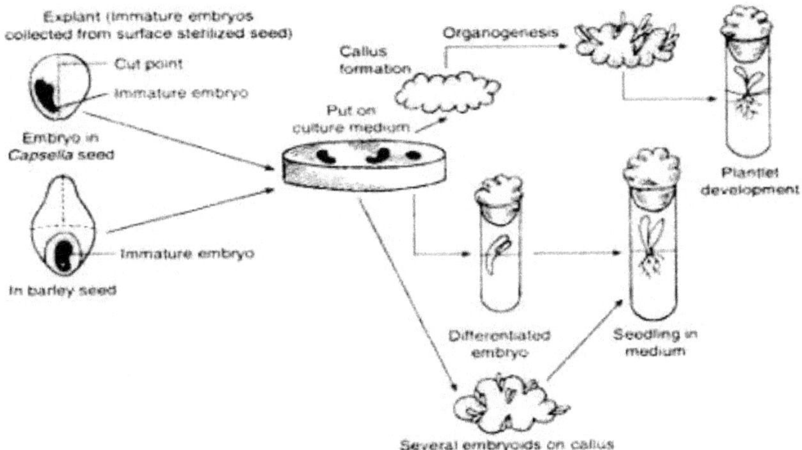

- o   Isolate immature or mature embryos aseptically.

- o   Inoculate onto MS medium with growth regulators.

- o   Maintain under light conditions to promote germination.

3. **Endosperm Culture:**

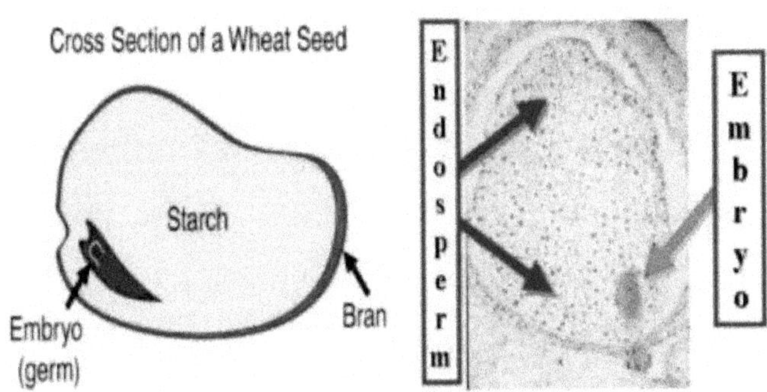

- o   Isolate endosperm tissue from seeds.

- o   Place onto MS medium with an appropriate combination of auxins and cytokinins.

- o Observe for callus formation and plantlet regeneration.

Results:

Successful formation of callus and plant regeneration from anther, embryo, and endosperm tissues.

Discussion Questions and Answers:

1. **What is the purpose of anther culture?**
   - o To produce haploid plants that can be used in plant breeding.
2. **Why is embryo culture important in tissue culture?**
   - o It is used for the rescue of immature embryos and propagation of rare species.
3. **What are the applications of endosperm culture?**
   - o It is used for producing triploid plants and genetic studies.
4. **What factors influence the success of anther culture?**
   - o The developmental stage of the anther, culture conditions, and media composition.
5. **How can contamination be prevented in embryo culture?**
   - o By following strict aseptic techniques during isolation and inoculation.

Experiment 56: Somatic Embryogenesis

Aim: To induce somatic embryogenesis from plant tissues under in vitro conditions.

Principle: Somatic embryogenesis is the process of developing somatic (non-reproductive) plant cells into embryos that can give rise to complete plants. This technique is widely used for plant propagation, genetic transformation, and conservation of germplasm.

Preparation of Reagents:

1. **Murashige and Skoog (MS) Medium:**
   - Macronutrients and micronutrients as per standard formulation.
   - Vitamins and sucrose (30 g/L).
   - Agar (8 g/L) for solid medium.
   - pH adjusted to 5.7.
2. **Growth Regulators:**
   - 2,4-D (Dichlorophenoxyacetic acid) - for callus induction.
   - BAP (6-Benzylaminopurine) - for shoot induction.
   - NAA (Naphthaleneacetic acid) - for root development.

Procedure:

1. **Callus Induction:**

- Select healthy explants such as leaf, stem, or root sections.
- Surface sterilize explants using ethanol (70%) and sodium hypochlorite (2-5%).
- Inoculate onto MS medium supplemented with 2,4-D (1-2 mg/L).
- Incubate under dark conditions at 25°C for 2-3 weeks.
- Observe callus formation.

2. **Embryo Formation:**
   - Transfer callus to embryogenic medium with reduced auxin and increased cytokinin levels.
   - Incubate under light conditions to promote embryo differentiation.
   - Observe for somatic embryo formation.

3. **Plantlet Regeneration:**
   - Transfer embryos to MS medium with appropriate growth regulators.
   - Monitor shoot and root development.

4. **Hardening:**

   Acclimatize regenerated plantlets to external conditions by gradually reducing humidity.

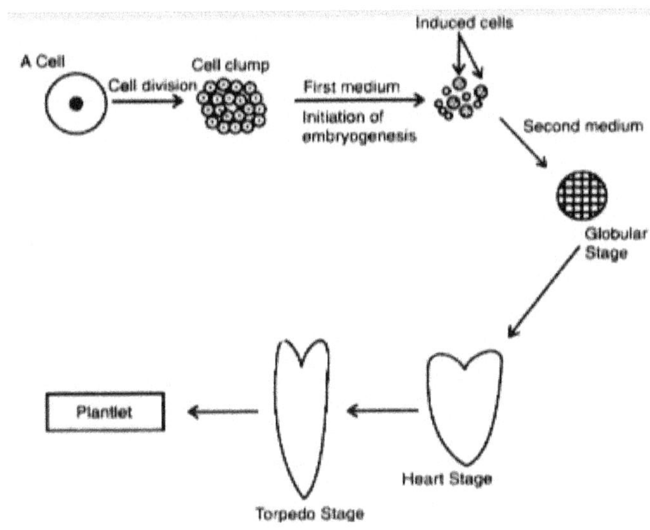

o

Results:

Formation of somatic embryos and their development into plantlets.

Discussion Questions and Answers:

1. **What is the significance of somatic embryogenesis?**
   - o It enables large-scale propagation and genetic improvement of plants.
2. **Which plant growth regulators are essential for somatic embryogenesis?**
   - o Auxins (e.g., 2,4-D) and cytokinins (e.g., BAP).
3. **Why is callus formation an essential step in somatic embryogenesis?**
   - o It serves as an intermediary stage for cell differentiation into embryos.

4. **What factors influence the efficiency of somatic embryogenesis?**

   - Type of explant, medium composition, and environmental conditions.

5. **How can somatic embryogenesis be applied in agriculture?**

   - It can be used for rapid propagation of elite plant varieties and germplasm conservation.

Experiment 57: Preparation of Synthetic Seeds by Sodium Alginate Method

Aim: To prepare synthetic seeds using the sodium alginate encapsulation method.

Principle: Synthetic seed technology involves encapsulating somatic embryos or other plant propagules in a protective gel, such as sodium alginate, to simulate natural seeds. This method allows for easy handling, transportation, and storage of plant material.

Preparation of Reagents:

1. **Sodium Alginate Solution:**
   a) Sodium alginate - 3% (w/v)
   b) Distilled water - up to 100 mL
2. **Calcium Chloride ($CaCl_2$) Solution:**
   a) $CaCl_2$ - 100 mM
   b) Distilled water - up to 100 mL
3. **Plant Material:** Somatic embryos or shoot tips

Procedure:

1. Prepare a 3% sodium alginate solution by dissolving sodium alginate in distilled water.
2. Prepare a 100 mM calcium chloride solution.
3. Suspend the plant propagules (e.g., somatic embryos) in the sodium alginate solution.

4. Using a sterile pipette, drop the alginate-encapsulated propagules into the calcium chloride solution.

5. Allow the beads to harden for 20-30 minutes.

6. Rinse the synthetic seeds with sterile distilled water.

7. Store the synthetic seeds in a sterile container under appropriate conditions.

Results:

The synthetic seeds formed will be firm, uniform gel beads containing plant propagules.

Discussion Questions and Answers:

1. **What are synthetic seeds?**
   - Synthetic seeds are artificially encapsulated plant propagules that can be stored and grown under controlled conditions.

2. **Why is sodium alginate used for encapsulation?**

- o Sodium alginate forms a gel matrix when exposed to calcium chloride, providing protection to the encapsulated propagules.

3. **What are the advantages of synthetic seeds?**

   - o They facilitate easy handling, transportation, and large-scale propagation of plant material.

4. **How long can synthetic seeds be stored?**

   - o Storage duration depends on the plant species and storage conditions, but they can typically be stored for several weeks to months.

5. **What are the potential applications of synthetic seeds?**

   - o They are used in germplasm conservation, large-scale propagation, and crop improvement programs.

Experiment 58: Isolation of Protoplasts

Aim: To isolate protoplasts from plant tissues for further culturing and regeneration.

Principle: Protoplasts are plant cells without a cell wall, isolated by enzymatic digestion. They provide a unique system for studying cell biology, genetic manipulation, and somatic hybridization.

Preparation of Reagents:

1. **Enzyme Solution:**
   a) Cellulase (2%)
   b) Pectinase (0.5%)
   c) Mannitol (0.4 M)
   d) Calcium chloride (10 mM)
   e) MES buffer (pH 5.8)

2. **Osmoticum Solution:**
   a) Mannitol (0.5 M)
   b) Sorbitol (0.5 M)
   c) pH adjusted to 5.8

3. **Washing Buffer:**
   a) Sucrose (0.6 M)
   b) pH adjusted to 5.8

Procedure:

1. Select healthy plant tissue and cut into small pieces.

2. Incubate in enzyme solution for 3-6 hours at 25°C with gentle shaking.

3. Filter the solution through a fine mesh to remove undigested tissue.

4. Centrifuge at low speed to collect the protoplasts.

5. Wash the protoplasts with osmoticum solution and resuspend in culture medium.

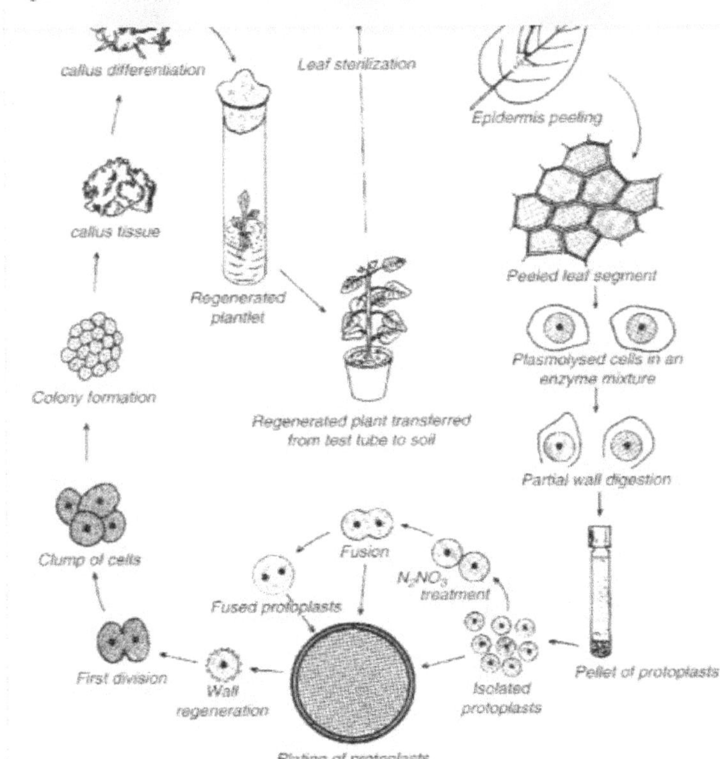

Results: The isolated protoplasts should appear spherical and viable under a microscope.

Discussion Questions and Answers:

1. **What is the significance of protoplast isolation?**
   - It facilitates genetic transformation and somatic hybridization.

2. **Why are enzymes used in protoplast isolation?**
   - They help digest the cell wall, releasing the protoplast.

3. **How can protoplast viability be assessed?**
   - By using vital stains such as fluorescein diacetate (FDA).

Experiment 59: Culturing of Protoplasts

Aim: To culture isolated protoplasts for cell wall regeneration and plant regeneration.

Principle: Cultured protoplasts can regenerate their cell walls, divide, and form callus, which can eventually develop into whole plants.

Preparation of Reagents:

1. **Protoplast Culture Medium:**

    a) Murashige and Skoog (MS) medium
    b) Sucrose (0.6 M)
    c) NAA (1 mg/L)
    d) BAP (0.5 mg/L)

2. **Agar Medium:** MS medium solidified with 0.8% agar

Procedure:

1. Embed the isolated protoplasts in a thin layer of agar medium.
2. Incubate under controlled conditions (25°C, 16 hours light/8 hours dark).
3. Observe for cell wall formation and cell division.
4. Transfer callus to regeneration medium for shoot and root formation.

Results:

Successful protoplast culture leads to the development of cell clusters, callus, and eventually plantlets.

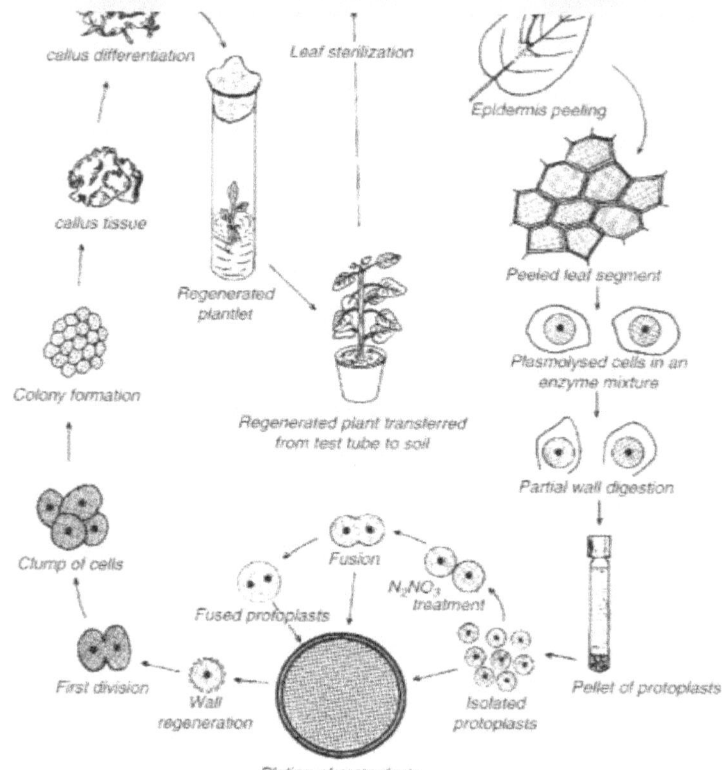

Discussion Questions and Answers:

1. **What factors influence protoplast culture success?**
   - Osmotic balance, nutrient composition, and hormonal concentration.
2. **Why is an osmoticum used in protoplast culture?**

o   To maintain protoplast integrity and prevent bursting.

3. How can protoplasts be induced to form callus?

o   By optimizing growth regulator concentrations in the medium.

Experiment 60: Preparation of Culture Media for Animal Cell Culture

Aim: To prepare culture media suitable for the growth and maintenance of animal cells in vitro.

Principle: Animal cell culture requires a nutrient-rich medium that provides essential nutrients, growth factors, and a suitable environment to support cell proliferation and maintenance. The culture medium should mimic the natural extracellular environment.

Preparation of Reagents:

1. **Dulbecco's Modified Eagle Medium (DMEM):**
   a) Glucose - 4.5 g/L
   b) L-Glutamine - 4 mM
   c) Sodium bicarbonate - 3.7 g/L
   d) pH adjusted to 7.2-7.4

2. **Fetal Bovine Serum (FBS):**
   a) Sterile filtered and heat inactivated
   b) Added at a concentration of 10%

3. **Antibiotics:**
   a) Penicillin (100 U/mL) and Streptomycin (100 µg/mL)

4. **Trypsin-EDTA Solution:**
   a) Trypsin (0.25%)
   b) EDTA (0.02%)

5. **Phosphate Buffered Saline (PBS):**
   a) NaCl - 8 g

b) KCl - 0.2 g

c) Na_2HPO_4 - 1.44 g

d) KH_2PO_4 - 0.24 g

e) Distilled water - up to 1 L

Procedure:

1. Prepare the DMEM medium by dissolving the required components in sterile distilled water.

2. Filter sterilize the prepared medium using a 0.22 μm membrane filter.

3. Supplement the medium with 10% FBS and antibiotics.

4. Store the medium at 4°C until use.

5. Warm the medium to 37°C before use in cell culture experiments.

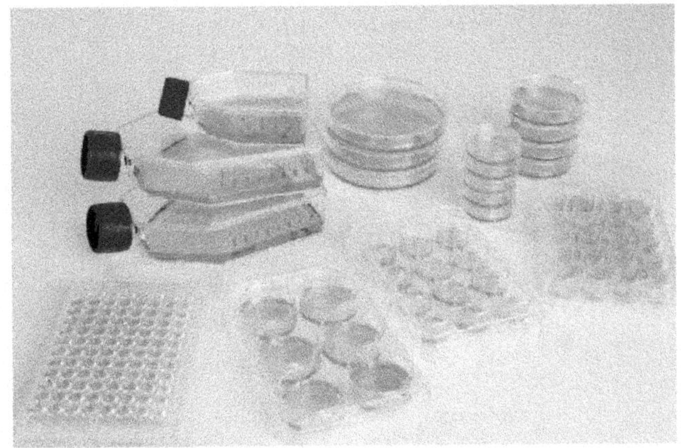

Results:

The prepared culture medium should be clear and free from contamination, providing optimal growth conditions for animal cells.

Discussion Questions and Answers:

1. **Why is FBS added to the culture medium?**
   - o FBS provides essential growth factors, hormones, and nutrients required for cell proliferation.
2. **Why is pH adjustment crucial for animal cell culture?**
   - o A pH of 7.2-7.4 is optimal for maintaining cellular functions and enzyme activities.
3. **What is the purpose of antibiotics in the culture medium?**
   - o To prevent bacterial and fungal contamination.
4. **Why is sterile filtration used in media preparation?**
   - o It removes contaminants and ensures sterility.
5. **What is the role of trypsin-EDTA in cell culture?**
   - o It helps detach adherent cells from the culture vessel surface.

Experiment 61: Primary Cell Culture Using Chick Embryo

Aim: To establish a primary cell culture from a chick embryo.

Principle: Primary cell culture involves the isolation of cells directly from tissues, retaining their original characteristics. Chick embryo cells are commonly used due to their rapid growth and adaptability to in vitro conditions.

Preparation of Reagents:

1. **Hank's Balanced Salt Solution (HBSS):**
    a) NaCl - 8 g
    b) KCl - 0.4 g
    c) Na_2HPO_4 - 0.06 g
    d) KH_2PO_4 - 0.06 g
    e) Glucose - 1 g
    f) Distilled water - up to 1 L
    g) Adjust pH to 7.2
2. **Trypsin-EDTA Solution:**
    a) Trypsin (0.25%)
    b) EDTA (0.02%)
3. **Complete Culture Medium:**
    a) Dulbecco's Modified Eagle Medium (DMEM)
    b) 10% Fetal Bovine Serum (FBS)
    c) Antibiotic solution (Penicillin/Streptomycin 100 U/mL)

4. **Sterile Phosphate Buffered Saline (PBS):** To wash tissue samples

Procedure:

1. **Dissection of Chick Embryo:**
   - Dissect a 10-day-old chick embryo under sterile conditions.
   - Collect tissue samples such as liver or heart.

2. **Tissue Disaggregation:**
   - Wash tissues with sterile PBS.
   - Mince tissue into small pieces.
   - Treat with trypsin-EDTA solution for 10-15 minutes to dissociate cells.

3. **Cell Collection:**
   - Centrifuge at 1000 rpm for 5 minutes to pellet the cells.
   - Resuspend cells in complete culture medium.

4. **Seeding Cells:**
   - Transfer cell suspension to a sterile culture flask.
   - Incubate at 37°C with 5% CO_2.

5. **Observation:**
   - Monitor cell adherence and growth under a microscope.

Results:

Successful cell attachment and proliferation will be observed, indicating the establishment of a primary cell culture.

Discussion Questions and Answers:

1. **Why is chick embryo used for primary cell culture?**
    - Chick embryos are rich in rapidly dividing cells and are easy to handle in laboratory settings.

2. **What is the role of trypsin-EDTA in cell isolation?**
    - It helps in breaking down cell-cell and cell-matrix adhesions, allowing cell dissociation.

3. **Why is CO_2 required in cell culture incubation?**
    - It helps maintain the pH of the culture medium.

4. **What precautions should be taken during cell culture?**
    - Maintain aseptic conditions to prevent contamination.

5. **How can cell viability be assessed?**
    - Using trypan blue exclusion assay to check for viable cells.

Experiment 62: Cell Passaging

Aim: To perform cell passaging to maintain healthy cell cultures and avoid over-confluency.

Principle: Cell passaging, also known as subculturing, involves transferring cells from a crowded culture vessel to a new vessel with fresh growth medium. This ensures optimal growth conditions and prevents contact inhibition.

Preparation of Reagents:

1. **Trypsin-EDTA Solution:**
    a) Trypsin (0.25%)
    b) EDTA (0.02%)
2. **Complete Culture Medium:**
    a) Dulbecco's Modified Eagle Medium (DMEM)
    b) 10% Fetal Bovine Serum (FBS)
    c) Antibiotic solution (Penicillin/Streptomycin 100 U/mL)
3. **Phosphate Buffered Saline (PBS):** To wash cells

Procedure:

1. Observe the cells under an inverted microscope to check confluency.
2. Aspirate the old culture medium and wash the cells with sterile PBS.
3. Add an appropriate volume of trypsin-EDTA solution and incubate for 2-5 minutes until cells detach.

4. Neutralize trypsin by adding an equal volume of complete culture medium.

5. Transfer the cell suspension to a sterile centrifuge tube and spin at 1000 rpm for 5 minutes.

6. Resuspend the cell pellet in fresh culture medium.

7. Seed the required number of cells into new culture flasks.

8. Incubate at 37°C with 5% CO_2.

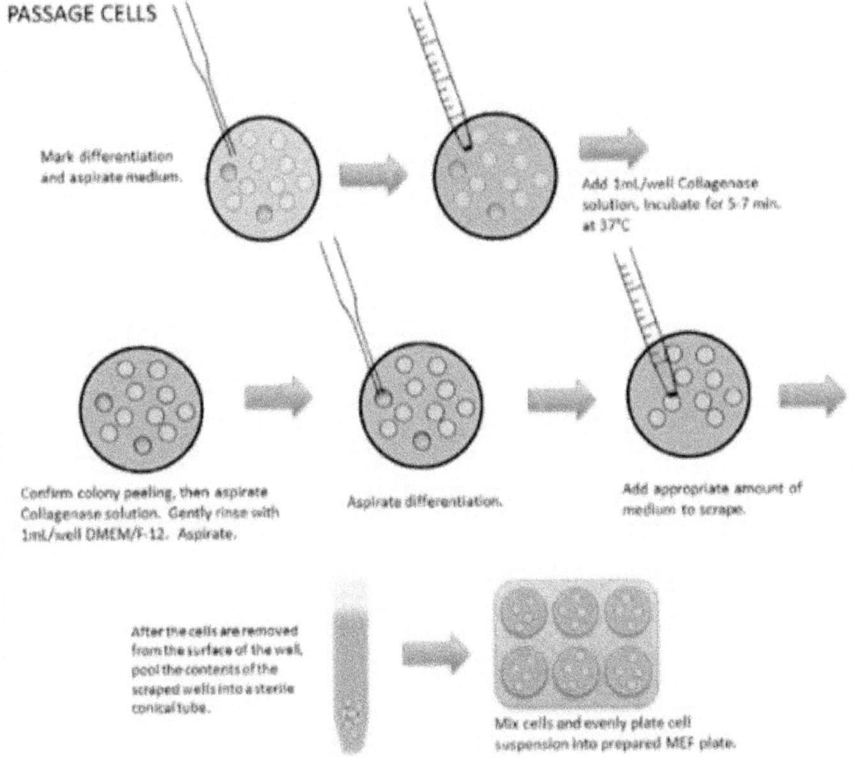

Results:

Healthy, evenly distributed cells will be observed in the new culture flasks.

Discussion Questions and Answers:

1. **Why is cell passaging necessary in cell culture?**
   - To maintain cell viability and prevent over-confluency.

2. **What is the role of trypsin in cell passaging?**
   - Trypsin helps detach adherent cells from the culture surface.

3. **Why is FBS added to the culture medium?**
   - It provides essential nutrients and neutralizes trypsin activity.

4. **What precautions should be taken during cell passaging?**
   - Maintain sterile conditions to avoid contamination.

5. **How often should cells be passaged?**
   - Depending on the cell type, usually every 2-4 days.

Experiment 63: Cryopreservation of Cells

Aim: To preserve cells at ultra-low temperatures for long-term storage.

Principle: Cryopreservation involves freezing cells in cryoprotective agents to prevent ice crystal formation and cellular damage, ensuring cell viability upon thawing.

Preparation of Reagents:

1. **Cryoprotective Medium:**
   - 10% Dimethyl Sulfoxide (DMSO)
   - 90% Fetal Bovine Serum (FBS)
2. **Liquid Nitrogen Storage:**
   - For storing cells at -196°C

Procedure:

1. Harvest cells by trypsinization and centrifugation.
2. Resuspend cells in cryoprotective medium.
3. Aliquot the cell suspension into cryovials.
4. Freeze gradually by placing in a -80°C freezer overnight.
5. Transfer to liquid nitrogen for long-term storage.

Results:

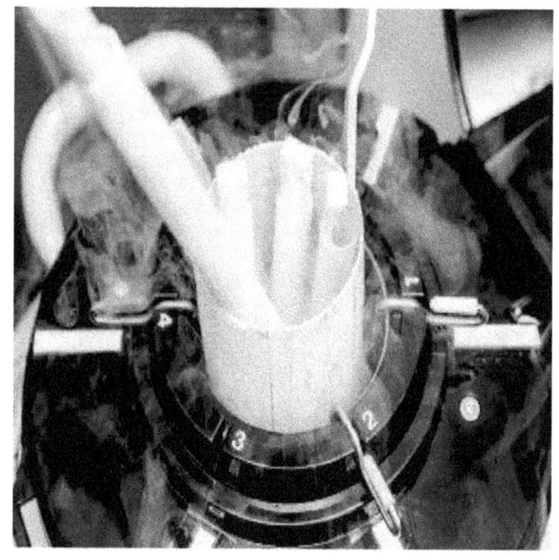

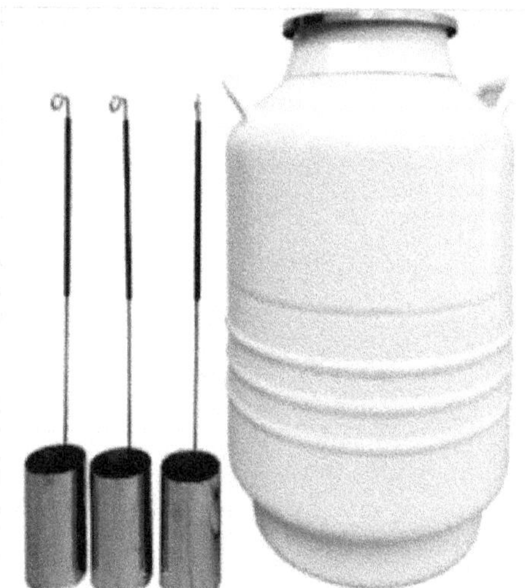

Viable cells should be recovered upon thawing and reculturing.

Discussion Questions and Answers:

1. **Why is DMSO used in cryopreservation?**

o   It prevents ice crystal formation that can damage cells.

2. **Why should cells be frozen gradually?**

    o   To prevent cellular shock and damage.

3. **What is the ideal temperature for long-term cell storage?**

    o   -196°C in liquid nitrogen.

Experiment 64: Revival of Cryopreserved Cells

Aim: To successfully revive cryopreserved cells and maintain their viability for further culture.

Principle: Revival of cryopreserved cells involves rapid thawing followed by gradual rehydration and seeding in a fresh culture medium to restore cellular functions and viability.

Preparation of Reagents:

1. **Complete Culture Medium:**

    a) Dulbecco's Modified Eagle Medium (DMEM)
    b) 10% Fetal Bovine Serum (FBS)
    c) Antibiotic solution (Penicillin/Streptomycin 100 U/mL)

2. **Phosphate Buffered Saline (PBS):** To wash cells

Procedure:

1. Remove cryovial from liquid nitrogen storage and quickly thaw in a 37°C water bath for 1-2 minutes until only a small ice pellet remains.
2. Transfer the thawed cell suspension to a sterile centrifuge tube containing pre-warmed complete culture medium.
3. Centrifuge at 1000 rpm for 5 minutes to pellet the cells.

4. Aspirate the supernatant and resuspend the cell pellet in fresh culture medium.

5. Seed the cells into a culture flask and incubate at 37°C with 5% CO_2.

6. Monitor cell attachment and viability under an inverted microscope.

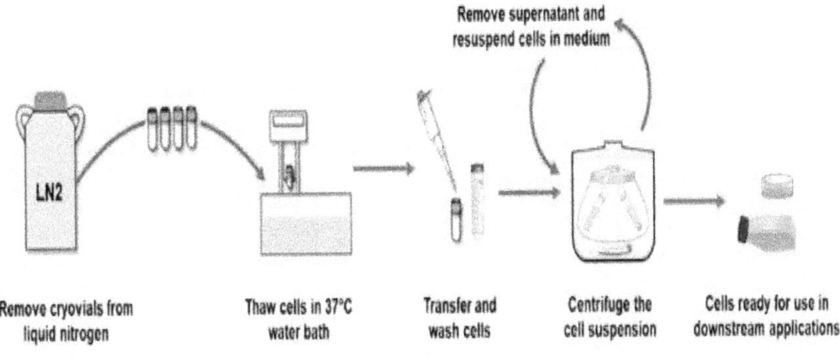

Results:

Viable, healthy cells should attach and proliferate within 24 hours of revival.

Discussion Questions and Answers:

1. **Why should cryopreserved cells be thawed quickly?**
   - Rapid thawing prevents ice crystal formation, which can damage cell membranes.

2. **Why is it important to remove cryoprotectant after thawing?**

- Cryoprotectants like DMSO can be toxic to cells if not removed promptly.

3. **What temperature is used for thawing cryopreserved cells?**

   - $37°C$ in a water bath.

4. **How can cell viability be assessed after revival?**

   - Using trypan blue exclusion assay to check for viable cells.

5. **What precautions should be taken during the revival process?**

   - Work quickly to avoid prolonged exposure to cryoprotectants and maintain sterility.

Experiment 65: Nuclear and Mitochondrial Staining of Cells

Aim: **To visualize and study the nucleus and mitochondria of cells using specific staining techniques.**

Principle: **Nuclear and mitochondrial staining are essential techniques in cell biology that allow the visualization of cellular structures using fluorescent or chromogenic dyes. Nuclear stains bind to DNA, highlighting the nucleus, while mitochondrial stains target specific components within mitochondria to observe their structure and distribution.**

Preparation of Reagents:

1. **DAPI (4',6-diamidino-2-phenylindole) Staining Solution:** DAPI (1 µg/mL in PBS)
2. **MitoTracker Staining Solution:** MitoTracker Red (200 nM in PBS)
3. **Phosphate Buffered Saline (PBS):** To wash cells

Procedure:

1. **Nuclear Staining with DAPI:**
   o Wash cells with PBS.
   o Add DAPI staining solution and incubate for 5-10 minutes in the dark.
   o Wash cells with PBS to remove excess stain.
   o Observe under a fluorescence microscope using a UV filter.

2. **Mitochondrial Staining with MitoTracker:**

   - Prepare live cells in culture.

   - Add MitoTracker staining solution to the culture medium.

   - Incubate for 30 minutes at 37°C.

   - Wash with PBS and observe under a fluorescence microscope using the appropriate filter

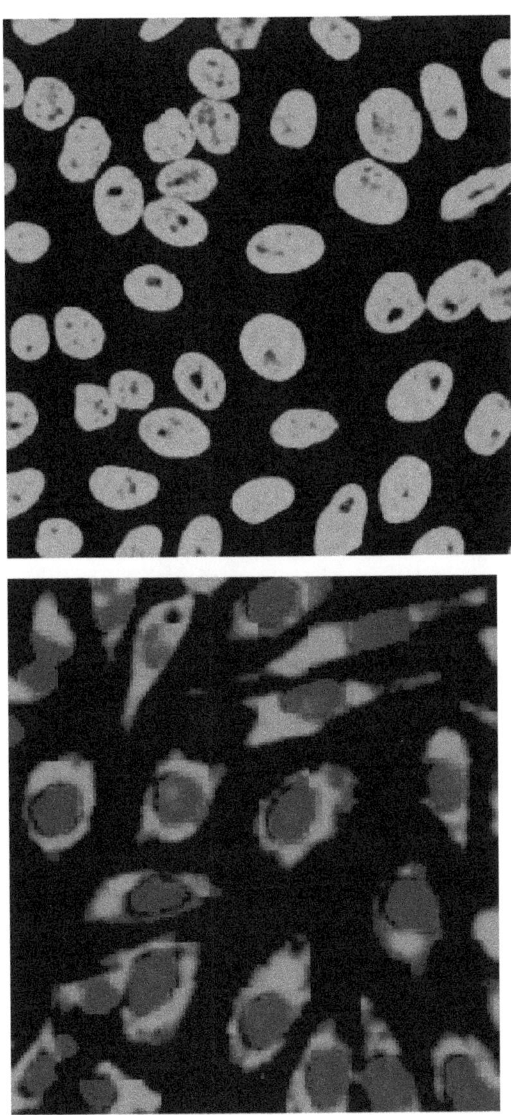

Nuclear staining will show bright blue fluorescence, and mitochondrial staining will show red fluorescence, indicating the presence and localization of the respective organelles.

Discussion Questions and Answers:

1. **What is the purpose of DAPI staining?**
   - To visualize the nucleus by binding specifically to DNA.

2. **Why is MitoTracker used for mitochondrial staining?**
   - It selectively accumulates in active mitochondria based on membrane potential.

3. **Why should staining procedures be done in the dark?**
   - To prevent photobleaching of fluorescent dyes.

4. **What microscope is used for observing stained cells?**
   - A fluorescence microscope.

5. **How does mitochondrial staining help in cell analysis?**
   - It helps study mitochondrial distribution, morphology, and function in live cells.

Experiment 66: Cell Viability Test

Aim: To assess the viability of cultured cells using the trypan blue exclusionmethod.

Principle: The trypan blue dye selectively stains non-viable cells with compromised membranes, while viable cells exclude the dye and remain unstained.

Preparation of Reagents:

1. Trypan Blue Solution (0.4%)
2. Phosphate Buffered Saline (PBS)
3. Complete Culture Medium

Procedure:

1. Harvest cells from the culture by trypsinization and centrifugation.
2. Resuspend cells in fresh culture medium.
3. Mix 10 µL of the cell suspension with 10 µL of trypan blue solution.
4. Load the mixture onto a hemocytometer.
5. Count both stained (non-viable) and unstained (viable) cells under a microscope.

Results:

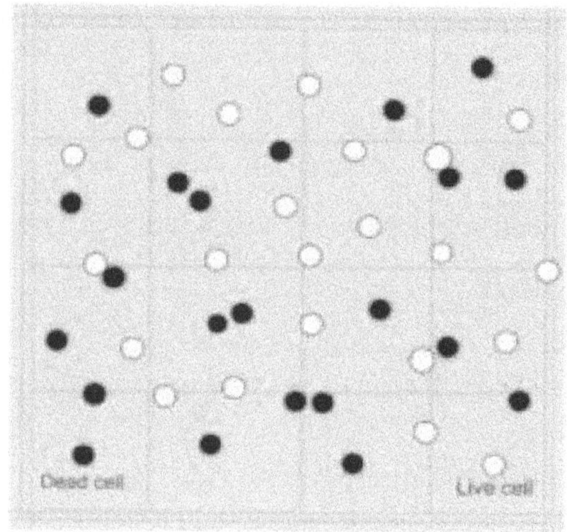

The percentage of viable cells is calculated using the formula:

Cell Viability (%) = (Number of viable cells / Total cells) × 100

Discussion Questions and Answers:

1. **Why is trypan blue used for cell viability testing?**
   - It differentiates live and dead cells based on membrane integrity.

2. **What is the significance of cell viability assessment?**
   - It helps determine cell health and suitability for experiments.

Experiment 67: Haemoglobin-Based Blood Substitutes

Aim: To understand the principles and applications of haemoglobin-based blood substitutes.

Principle: Haemoglobin-based blood substitutes (HBOCs) are designed to mimic the oxygen-carrying function of natural haemoglobin. These substitutes are used as an alternative to donor blood, particularly in emergency and surgical situations where blood transfusions are limited.

Preparation of Reagents:

1. **Purified Haemoglobin Solution:**
   a) Haemoglobin (bovine or recombinant human)
   b) Phosphate buffer (pH 7.4)
   c) Antioxidants to prevent oxidation

2. **Stabilizing Agents:**
   a) Polyethylene glycol (PEG)
   b) Dextran

3. **Oxygen-Carrying Buffer:**
   a) Balanced salt solution
   b) pH adjusted to 7.4

Procedure:

1. Prepare haemoglobin solution by dissolving purified haemoglobin in phosphate buffer.
2. Add stabilizing agents such as PEG to increase molecular stability and circulation time.

3. Filter sterilize the solution to remove any contaminants.

4. Test oxygen-carrying capacity using oxygen dissociation curves.

5. Store the prepared blood substitute at 4°C until use.

Results: Haemoglobin-based blood substitutes should retain their oxygen-carrying capacity and show stability over a defined period.

Discussion Questions and Answers:

1. **What are the advantages of haemoglobin-based blood substitutes?**

   ➢ They provide an immediate oxygen supply and have a longer shelf life compared to donor blood.

2. **What are the potential risks associated with HBOCs?**

   ➢ They may cause oxidative stress and hypertension due to free haemoglobin toxicity.

3. **Why are stabilizing agents used in haemoglobin substitutes?**

   ➢ To prevent haemoglobin breakdown and prolong circulation time.

4. **How are haemoglobin-based substitutes tested for effectiveness?**

   ➢ By measuring their oxygen dissociation curves and hemolysis rates.

5. **What are the applications of haemoglobin-based blood substitutes?**

➢ They are used in trauma care, military applications, and regions with limited blood supply.

68. Viva Voce Questions and Answers

1.   What is the principle of the Biuret test for protein estimation?

The Biuret test is based on the reaction of peptide bonds in proteins with copper sulfate in an alkaline solution, forming a violet-colored complex.

2.   What is the role of Benedict's reagent in carbohydrate testing?

Benedict's reagent is used to detect reducing sugars, which reduce cupric ions to cuprous oxide, forming a red precipitate.

3.   Why is SDS used in protein electrophoresis?

SDS (Sodium Dodecyl Sulfate) denatures proteins and provides them with a uniform negative charge, allowing separation based on molecular weight.

4.   What is the principle behind the Lowry's method for protein estimation?

It involves the reaction of proteins with the Folin-Ciocalteu reagent, leading to a color change measurable at 750 nm.

5.   What is the significance of Gram staining?

It differentiates bacteria into Gram-positive and Gram-negative based on cell wall composition.

6.   What is the role of EDTA in DNA isolation?

EDTA chelates divalent cations, inhibiting DNase activity and preventing DNA degradation.

7.   What are the different types of chromatography used in biotechnology?

Paper chromatography, thin-layer chromatography (TLC), gas chromatography (GC), and high-performance liquid chromatography (HPLC).

8. What is the purpose of using iodine in starch detection?

Iodine forms a blue-black complex with starch, indicating its presence.

9. What are plasmids?

Plasmids are small, circular DNA molecules that can replicate independently within bacterial cells and are commonly used in genetic engineering.

10. What is the function of restriction enzymes?

Restriction enzymes cut DNA at specific recognition sequences, facilitating genetic manipulation.

11. What are the four phases of bacterial growth?

Lag phase, log (exponential) phase, stationary phase, and death phase.

12. What is the purpose of cell fractionation?

To isolate different cellular components such as nuclei, mitochondria, and cytoplasm for further analysis.

13. What is the principle of the Bradford protein assay?

It involves the binding of Coomassie Brilliant Blue dye to proteins, causing a color change measurable at 595 nm.

14. Why is aseptic technique important in microbiology?

It prevents contamination and ensures the accuracy of experimental results.

15. What is the purpose of an autoclave in the laboratory?

It sterilizes equipment and media using steam under high pressure.

16.   What is the principle of the orcinol test for RNA estimation?

Orcinol reacts with pentose sugars in RNA, forming a green color measurable at 660 nm.

17.   What are the applications of ELISA?

ELISA is used for detecting and quantifying antigens or antibodies in a sample

18.   What is the difference between DNA and RNA?

DNA is double-stranded and contains deoxyribose sugar and thymine, whereas RNA is single-stranded and contains ribose sugar and uracil.

19.   What is the role of primers in PCR?

Primers are short DNA sequences that initiate DNA synthesis during PCR.

20.   What are the basic steps of PCR?

Denaturation, annealing, and extension.

21.   Why is the Ames test used in microbiology? It assesses the mutagenic potential of chemical compounds.

22.   What is the principle of thin-layer chromatography (TLC)?

TLC separates components of a mixture based on their differential affinities to the stationary and mobile phases.

23.   What are monoclonal antibodies?

Monoclonal antibodies are identical antibodies produced by a single clone of B cells and specific to a single antigen.

24.   Why is glycerol used in cryopreservation?

Glycerol acts as a cryoprotectant, preventing the formation of ice crystals that can damage cells.

25.   What is the purpose of a hemocytometer?

It is used for counting cells in a known volume of liquid.

26.   What is the significance of Koch's postulates?

They establish a relationship between a microorganism and a disease by fulfilling specific criteria.

27.   What are secondary metabolites?

Secondary metabolites are organic compounds not directly involved in growth but important for defense and interaction with the environment.

28.   What is the purpose of Southern blotting?

It detects specific DNA sequences by hybridization with a labeled probe.

29.   What is quorum sensing in bacteria?

A communication mechanism that regulates gene expression in response to cell population density.

30.   What is the function of mitochondria in the cell?

Mitochondria generate ATP through oxidative phosphorylation, serving as the powerhouse of the cell.

31.   What is the purpose of Western blotting?

Western blotting is used to detect specific proteins in a sample using antibodies after separation by SDS-PAGE.

32.   What is the principle of Fehling's test?

Fehling's test detects reducing sugars by reducing cupric ions to cuprous oxide, resulting in a red precipitate.

33.   What are the applications of microbial culture?

Microbial cultures are used in antibiotic production, food fermentation, water quality testing, and biotechnology research.

34.   Why is phenol used in DNA extraction?

Phenol denatures proteins and separates them from nucleic acids during DNA extraction.

35.   What are transgenic organisms?

Transgenic organisms are genetically modified to contain foreign DNA that provides new traits.

36.   What is the principle of the Ninhydrin test?

Ninhydrin reacts with free amino acids to produce a deep purple color due to the formation of Ruhemann's purple.

37.   What is the function of ribosomes in cells?

Ribosomes synthesize proteins by translating mRNA into polypeptide chains.

38.   What is the significance of microbial colony counting?

Colony counting helps in estimating the concentration of viable microorganisms in a sample.

39.   What is the role of sodium carbonate in Benedict's test?

Sodium carbonate provides an alkaline medium required for the reduction of copper ions.

40.   What are the characteristics of Gram-positive bacteria?

Gram-positive bacteria have a thick peptidoglycan cell wall and retain the crystal violet stain.

41.   Why is solid media preferred over liquid media in some microbial studies?

Solid media allow the isolation of individual colonies and the study of colony morphology.

42.   What is the purpose of the catalase test?

The catalase test detects the presence of the catalase enzyme, which breaks down hydrogen peroxide into water and oxygen.

43.   What are the applications of PCR in disease diagnosis?

PCR is used to detect genetic mutations, pathogens, and viruses in clinical samples.

44.   What is the difference between isotonic, hypertonic, and hypotonic solutions?

Isotonic solutions have equal osmotic pressure, hypertonic solutions have higher osmotic pressure, and hypotonic solutions have lower osmotic pressure.

45.   What is the principle of the iodine test for starch?

Iodine reacts with starch to form a blue-black complex, indicating the presence of starch.

46.   What is the role of magnesium ions in PCR?

Magnesium ions act as a cofactor for DNA polymerase, enabling efficient DNA synthesis.

47.   What is the significance of micropropagation?

Micropropagation allows the mass production of disease-free plants under controlled conditions.

48.   What is the function of DNA helicase?

DNA helicase unwinds the DNA double helix during replication.

49.   Why is blood smear staining important in hematology?

It allows the visualization and identification of different blood cell types for diagnostic purposes.

50.   What are the main differences between competitive and non-competitive enzyme inhibition?

Competitive inhibition involves binding at the active site, while non-competitive inhibition binds to a different site and alters enzyme activity.

51. What is the purpose of mounting Barr bodies?

To observe the inactivated X chromosome in female cells, aiding in genetic studies.

52. What are the advantages of using animal cell culture in research   It provides a controlled environment for studying cell behavior, drug testing, and genetic manipulation.

53. What is the role of sodium hypochlorite in surface sterilization?

It acts as a disinfectant by killing bacteria and fungi on surfaces.

54. Why is acetone used in lipid extraction?

Acetone dissolves lipids efficiently, helping in their separation from other biomolecules.

55. What is the principle of the indole test?

The indole test detects the breakdown of tryptophan to produce indole, which forms a red complex with Kovac's reagent.

56. What are the benefits of using synthetic seeds?

Synthetic seeds help in easy storage, transportation, and propagation of plant tissues.

57. Why is sodium dodecyl sulfate (SDS) used in protein extraction?

SDS solubilizes proteins by disrupting their hydrophobic interactions and denaturing them.

58. What is the significance of endospore staining?

•   Endospore staining helps in the identification of spore-forming bacteria, such as Bacillus and Clostridium species.

59.   What are the applications of flow cytometry?

Flow cytometry is used to analyze cell size, complexity, and fluorescence in cell sorting and diagnostics.

60.   What is the principle of the Methyl Red (MR) test?The MR test detects the production of stable acids from glucose fermentation, indicated by a red color at acidic pH.

61.   What is the significance of protein denaturation?

Protein denaturation disrupts the secondary and tertiary structure of proteins, leading to loss of function.

62.   What is the purpose of performing serial dilution in microbiology?

Serial dilution helps to reduce the concentration of microorganisms to obtain countable colonies.

63.   What is the function of a spectrophotometer in nucleic acid analysis?

It measures the absorbance of nucleic acids at 260 nm to determine their concentration and purity.

64.   What are the main functions of carbohydrates in living organisms?

Carbohydrates provide energy, serve as structural components, and participate in cell signaling.

65.   What is the role of Taq polymerase in PCR   Taq polymerase is a heat-stable enzyme that synthesizes DNA strands during the extension phase of PCR.

66.   What is the difference between batch and continuous fermentation?

In batch fermentation, nutrients are supplied at the start, whereas in continuous fermentation, nutrients are continuously supplied.

67.   What are the functions of lipids in biological membranes?

Lipids provide structural integrity, serve as barriers, and facilitate cell signaling.

68.   Why is the Voges-Proskauer (VP) test performed in microbiology?

The VP test detects acetoin production from glucose fermentation, indicating the presence of certain bacteria.

69.   What is the significance of antigen-antibody interactions in immunology?

These interactions are crucial for immune defense and diagnostic applications such as ELISA.

70.   What are the key steps involved in DNA isolation from plant tissues?

Cell lysis, removal of proteins and contaminants, DNA precipitation, and purification.

71.   What are the limitations of the DNS method for glucose estimation?

It is not specific to glucose and can react with other reducing sugars, leading to overestimation.

72.   What is the principle behind the citrate utilization test?

It tests the ability of bacteria to utilize citrate as the sole carbon source, leading to a color change in the medium.

73.   What are the differences between aerobic and anaerobic respiration?

Aerobic respiration requires oxygen, while anaerobic respiration occurs in its absence, producing less ATP.

74.   Why are fluorophores used in fluorescence microscopy?

Fluorophores emit light at specific wavelengths, allowing visualization of cellular structures.

75.   What is the purpose of performing a blank in spectrophotometry?

A blank is used to calibrate the spectrophotometer and eliminate background absorbance.

76.   What is the principle of affinity chromatography?

Affinity chromatography separates biomolecules based on their specific interactions with ligands attached to the stationary phase.

77.   What are the advantages of using recombinant DNA technology?

It allows the production of therapeutic proteins, genetically modified organisms, and enhanced agricultural crops.

78.   What is the importance of using control samples in an experiment?

Controls help validate the accuracy and reliability of experimental results.

79.   Why is the pH of culture media important for microbial growth?

Microbes have optimal pH ranges for growth, and deviations can inhibit metabolism and reproduction.

80.   What is the principle of the starch hydrolysis test?

It detects amylase activity by the disappearance of starch upon iodine staining.

81.   What is the significance of gel electrophoresis in proteomics?

It allows the separation and analysis of proteins based on their size and charge.

82.   What are the applications of microbial biofilms?

Biofilms are used in wastewater treatment, bioremediation, and industrial processes.

83.   What is the purpose of using selective media in microbiology?

Selective media promote the growth of specific microorganisms while inhibiting others.

84.   What are the differences between intrinsic and extrinsic factors affecting enzyme activity?

Intrinsic factors include enzyme structure and binding sites, while extrinsic factors include temperature and pH.

85.   What are the uses of recombinant insulin in medicine?

Recombinant insulin is used to manage diabetes by regulating blood glucose levels.

86.   What is the role of sodium hydroxide in the preparation of Fehling's solution?

Sodium hydroxide provides an alkaline environment necessary for the reaction to occur.

87.   What is the purpose of staining techniques in microbiology?

Staining enhances visualization of microbial cells and their components under a microscope.

88.   What is the function of the control DNA in PCR?

Control DNA serves as a reference to ensure that the PCR process is working correctly.

89.   Why is the exposure plate method used in air microbiology?

It helps in assessing airborne microbial contamination in different environments.

90.   What is the role of agar in solid culture media?

Agar provides a solid support for microbial growth and does not interfere with nutrient availability.

91. What is the significance of plasmid curing in bacteria?

Plasmid curing removes plasmids from bacterial cells to study their role in various traits such as antibiotic resistance.

92. What are the different methods of cell disruption for protein extraction?

Mechanical (homogenization, sonication), chemical (detergents, enzymes), and physical (freeze-thaw cycles) methods.

93. What is the purpose of performing the coagulase test in microbiology?

The coagulase test differentiates Staphylococcus aureus from other Staphylococcus species by detecting the enzyme that clots plasma.

94. What are the main components of Murashige and Skoog (MS) media?

Macronutrients, micronutrients, vitamins, plant growth regulators, and a carbon source.

95. What is the principle of the acetyl number determination of lipids?

It measures the number of hydroxyl groups present in fats and oils by acetylation and titration.

96. What is the function of an inoculating loop in microbiology?

It is used to transfer microorganisms under aseptic conditions without contamination.

97. What are the primary sources of contamination in cell culture?

Bacteria, fungi, viruses, and cross-contamination from other cell lines.

98.   What is the difference between qualitative and quantitative analysis in biotechnology   Qualitative analysis identifies components, while quantitative analysis determines their concentration.

99.   What is the purpose of using protein markers in SDS-PAGE?

Protein markers act as molecular weight standards to estimate the size of unknown proteins.

100.   What are the roles of antioxidants in biological systems?

 Antioxidants neutralize free radicals, protecting cells from oxidative damage.

101.   What is the role of DNA methylation in gene regulation?

- DNA methylation represses gene expression by modifying cytosine residues in DNA.

102.   What are the basic steps of bacterial transformation?

- Competence induction, uptake of foreign DNA, and expression of the introduced gene.

103.   What is the principle of the hydrogen sulfide (H_2S) strip test in water analysis?

- It detects the presence of sulfur-reducing bacteria that produce H_2S gas, turning the strip black.

104.   What are the primary applications of somatic embryogenesis?

- It is used for plant propagation, genetic modification, and germplasm preservation.

105.   What is the difference between antigen and hapten?

- An antigen induces an immune response, while a hapten requires a carrier molecule to become immunogenic.

106. What is the importance of immobilized enzymes in biotechnology?

- They offer improved stability, reusability, and controlled reaction conditions.

107. What are the different types of blotting techniques used in molecular biology?

- Southern blotting (DNA), Northern blotting (RNA), and Western blotting (protein).

108. What is the purpose of staining bacterial endospores?

- To identify spore-forming bacteria and assess their resistance to adverse conditions.

109. What are the major applications of tissue culture in plant biotechnology?

- Clonal propagation, production of secondary metabolites, and conservation of rare species.

110. What is the purpose of electrophoresis in nucleic acid analysis?

- It separates nucleic acids based on their size and charge for visualization and quantification.

111. What is the role of chlorophyll in photosynthesis?

- Chlorophyll absorbs light energy to drive the synthesis of ATP and NADPH during photosynthesis.

112. What is the function of a fume hood in a biotechnology lab?

- It provides ventilation to remove hazardous fumes and protect the user from exposure.

113.   What is the principle of the starch hydrolysis test in microbiology?

- It determines the presence of amylase by the hydrolysis of starch, indicated by a clear zone around the bacterial growth.

114.   Why are laminar airflow hoods used in microbiology labs?

- They provide a sterile working environment by directing filtered air in a uniform flow.

115.   What are the advantages of using synthetic seeds in agriculture?

- They facilitate easy handling, long-term storage, and large-scale propagation of elite plant varieties.

116.   What is the principle of the citrate utilization test in microbiology?

- It tests the ability of bacteria to use citrate as a carbon source, leading to color change in the medium.

117.   What are the key features of an ideal microbial growth medium?

- It should provide essential nutrients, maintain pH, and support optimal microbial growth.

118.   What is the purpose of performing the MTT assay in cell culture?

- The MTT assay assesses cell viability by measuring mitochondrial activity.

119.   What is the difference between natural and synthetic media in microbiology?

- Natural media contain undefined components, while synthetic media have precisely known compositions.

120.   What is the purpose of culturing microbes on selective media?

- Selective media promote the growth of specific microorganisms while inhibiting unwanted microbes.

121.   What is the significance of using hemocytometer in cell culture?

- A hemocytometer helps to determine cell concentration and viability in a given volume of liquid.

122.   What are the different types of microbial motility?

- Bacterial motility includes flagellar, gliding, twitching, and Brownian movement.

123.   What is the function of the sodium-potassium pump in cells?

- It maintains cell membrane potential by actively transporting sodium out and potassium into the cell.

124.   What is the importance of aseptic technique in cell culture?

- Aseptic techniques prevent contamination and maintain the integrity of cell cultures.

125.   What are the major applications of monoclonal antibodies?

- They are used in diagnostics, therapeutics, and research for targeted treatment and detection.

126.   What is the principle behind bacterial capsule staining?

- Capsule staining highlights the polysaccharide capsule surrounding bacterial cells, using negative staining techniques.

127.   What are the advantages of plant tissue culture over traditional propagation?

- Faster multiplication, disease-free plants, and year-round availability.

128. What are the different types of immunoassays used in diagnostics?

- ELISA, radioimmunoassay (RIA), and lateral flow assays.

129. What is the principle of the urease test?

- The urease test detects urease enzyme activity by converting urea into ammonia, raising the pH and changing the indicator color.

130. What is the role of bioinformatics in biotechnology?

- It involves the analysis of biological data, including genomics, proteomics, and drug discovery.

131. What are the key differences between prokaryotic and eukaryotic transcription?

- Prokaryotic transcription occurs in the cytoplasm and lacks post-transcriptional modifications, while eukaryotic transcription occurs in the nucleus with splicing and capping.

132. What is the purpose of using methylene blue in microbiology?

- It is used as a staining dye to visualize cells and test for the viability of cells.

133. What are the applications of gas chromatography (GC) in biotechnology?

- It is used for analyzing volatile compounds in environmental, food, and pharmaceutical industries.

134. What is the principle of the oxidase test in microbiology?

- It detects cytochrome c oxidase enzyme in bacteria by producing a color change upon oxidation.

135. Why is sodium citrate used in blood collection tubes?

- Sodium citrate prevents blood clotting by chelating calcium ions.

136.	What are the different types of vectors used in genetic engineering?

- Plasmids, bacteriophages, cosmids, and yeast artificial chromosomes (YACs).

137.	What is the purpose of gel documentation systems in molecular biology?

- They are used to capture and analyze gel electrophoresis results for nucleic acid and protein studies.

138.	What is the importance of biofilms in healthcare settings?

- Biofilms contribute to antibiotic resistance and persistent infections on medical devices.

139.	What are the components of a basic bacterial growth medium?

- Carbon source, nitrogen source, salts, vitamins, and pH buffers.

140.	What is the difference between differential and selective media?

- Differential media distinguish between organisms based on metabolic differences, while selective media allow the growth of specific organisms while inhibiting others.

141.	What is the significance of using spectrophotometry in enzyme kinetics?

- It helps measure reaction rates by monitoring changes in absorbance over time.

142.	What is the purpose of the nitrate reduction test?

- It detects the ability of bacteria to reduce nitrate to nitrite or other nitrogenous compounds.

143.	What are the advantages of using immobilized cells in bioprocessing?

- Improved stability, reusability, and ease of separation from the reaction medium.

146. What is the role of surfactants in cell lysis?

- Surfactants disrupt cell membranes by breaking lipid-lipid and lipid-protein interactions.

145. What are the factors affecting microbial growth?

- Temperature, pH, nutrient availability, oxygen levels, and moisture content.

146. Why is reverse transcription performed in molecular biology?

- Reverse transcription converts RNA into complementary DNA (cDNA) for further analysis, such as PCR.

147. What is the principle of enzyme-linked immunosorbent assay (ELISA)?

- It is based on the binding of an antigen to a specific antibody, followed by enzyme-mediated signal detection.

148. What are the types of restriction enzymes?

- Type I (random cuts), Type II (specific cuts), and Type III (cleave at sites near the recognition sequence).

149. What is the importance of DNA sequencing in biotechnology?

- DNA sequencing helps in understanding genetic information, identifying mutations, and developing targeted therapies.

150. What is the significance of quorum sensing in bacterial populations?

- Quorum sensing regulates bacterial gene expression in response to population density, influencing virulence and biofilm formation.

151.   What is the role of peptidoglycan in bacterial cell walls?

- Peptidoglycan provides structural support and rigidity to bacterial cell walls.

152.   What are the differences between light and electron microscopy?

- Light microscopy uses visible light to observe specimens, while electron microscopy uses electron beams for higher resolution imaging.

153.   What is the principle of atomic absorption spectroscopy (AAS)?

- AAS measures the concentration of metal ions in a sample by detecting the absorption of light at specific wavelengths.

154.   Why is ampicillin commonly used in plasmid selection?

- Ampicillin resistance is a selectable marker in plasmids, allowing the growth of transformed cells while inhibiting non-transformed cells.

155.   What are the different methods used for bacterial gene transfer?

- Transformation, transduction, and conjugation.

156.   What is the importance of blood typing in clinical diagnostics?

- Blood typing prevents transfusion reactions and ensures compatibility in blood transfusions.

157.   What is the function of chaperone proteins in cells?

- Chaperones assist in protein folding and prevent aggregation of misfolded proteins.

158.   What are the advantages of using fluorometers over spectrophotometers?

- Fluorometers provide higher sensitivity and specificity for detecting low concentrations of fluorescent compounds.

159.   What is the principle of immunoprecipitation?

- It isolates a specific antigen using an antibody that forms an immune complex, which can be precipitated and analyzed.

160.   What is the purpose of the thioglycolate broth in microbiology?

- It is used to determine the oxygen requirements of microorganisms.

161.   What is the importance of RNA splicing in eukaryotic cells?

- RNA splicing removes introns and joins exons to form a mature mRNA transcript for protein synthesis.

162.   What are the different types of mutations in DNA?

- Point mutations, insertions, deletions, and frameshift mutations.

163.   What is the significance of microbial bioleaching?

- Microbial bioleaching is used to extract metals from ores through biological processes.

164.   What is quorum sensing and how does it impact bacterial behavior?

- Quorum sensing allows bacteria to coordinate gene expression based on population density.

165.   What is the function of ribosomal RNA (rRNA)?

- rRNA is a key component of ribosomes and plays a role in translating mRNA into proteins.

166.   What is the significance of prebiotic and probiotic foods?

- Prebiotics promote beneficial gut bacteria, while probiotics contain live beneficial microorganisms.

167.   What is the function of chloroplast DNA in plants?

- It encodes essential genes for photosynthesis and other metabolic processes.

168.   What is the difference between competitive and uncompetitive enzyme inhibition?

- Competitive inhibitors bind to the active site, while uncompetitive inhibitors bind only to the enzyme-substrate complex.

169.   Why is it important to maintain sterility in pharmaceutical manufacturing?

- To prevent contamination and ensure product safety and efficacy.

170.   What is the role of lysozyme in bacterial cell lysis?

- Lysozyme breaks down peptidoglycan, leading to cell lysis in bacteria.

171.   What are exons and introns in eukaryotic genes?

- Exons code for proteins, while introns are non-coding sequences that are removed during RNA processing.

172.   What is the purpose of the Southern blot technique?

- It detects specific DNA sequences by hybridization with a complementary probe.

173.   What are the different types of bacterial plasmids?

- Conjugative plasmids, resistance plasmids, and virulence plasmids.

174.   What is the role of alkali lysis in plasmid DNA extraction?

- It disrupts bacterial cells and releases plasmid DNA while denaturing chromosomal DNA and proteins.

175.   What is the principle of HPLC in biotechnology?

- HPLC separates, identifies, and quantifies compounds based on their interactions with the stationary and mobile phases.

176.   Why is buffer capacity important in biochemical reactions?

- Buffer capacity ensures stable pH conditions to maintain enzyme activity and reaction rates.

177.   What are the applications of recombinant DNA technology in agriculture?

- Development of pest-resistant crops, improved yield, and stress tolerance.

178.   What is the function of lysosomes in eukaryotic cells?

- Lysosomes contain digestive enzymes that break down cellular waste and foreign materials.

179.   What are the different staining methods used for bacteria?

- Gram staining, acid-fast staining, capsule staining, and endospore staining.

180.   What is the significance of the Ames test in mutagenicity screening?

- The Ames test identifies chemical compounds that can cause mutations in DNA.

181.   What are the advantages of using hybridoma technology?

- It allows the production of specific, high-affinity monoclonal antibodies in large quantities.

182.   What is the role of cytokines in the immune system?

- Cytokines are signaling molecules that regulate immune responses and inflammation.

183. What is the function of restriction-modification systems in bacteria?

- They protect bacterial DNA from foreign genetic material by degrading unmodified DNA.

184. What are the different types of sequencing technologies used in genomics?

- Sanger sequencing, next-generation sequencing (NGS), and third-generation sequencing.

185. What is the purpose of using cryoprotectants in cell preservation?

- Cryoprotectants prevent ice crystal formation and cell damage during freezing.

186. What is the principle of northern blotting?

- Northern blotting detects specific RNA sequences by hybridization with a labeled probe.

187. What is the difference between totipotent and pluripotent cells?

- Totipotent cells can develop into any cell type, while pluripotent cells can develop into most but not all cell types.

188. What are the different phases of the cell cycle?

- G1 phase, S phase, G2 phase, and M phase (mitosis).

189. What is the purpose of polymerase chain reaction (PCR)?

- PCR amplifies DNA sequences for genetic analysis, diagnosis, and research purposes.

190. What are bioindicators and their applications in environmental monitoring?

- Bioindicators are organisms used to assess environmental health, such as pollution levels.

191.   What is the role of coenzymes in metabolism?

- Coenzymes act as carriers of electrons or functional groups in metabolic reactions.

192.   What is the function of mitochondria in apoptosis?

- Mitochondria release cytochrome c, which triggers the apoptotic cascade leading to programmed cell death.

193.   What is the purpose of quorum sensing inhibitors?

- They prevent bacteria from communicating and forming biofilms, reducing their pathogenicity.

194.   What are the characteristics of an ideal antimicrobial agent?

- Selective toxicity, broad-spectrum activity, low resistance development, and minimal side effects.

195.   What is the role of phytohormones in plant growth and development?

- Phytohormones regulate growth, development, and responses to environmental stimuli.

196.   What is the function of cytochrome P450 enzymes in drug metabolism?

- They catalyze the oxidation of drugs and toxins to facilitate their elimination.

197.   What is the significance of water activity in food microbiology?

- Water activity influences microbial growth and food spoilage.

198.   What is the role of reverse transcriptase in retroviruses?

- Reverse transcriptase converts viral RNA into DNA for integration into the host genome.

199. What are biosensors and their applications in biotechnology?

- Biosensors detect biological molecules and are used in medical diagnostics and environmental monitoring.

200. What is the function of histones in eukaryotic chromatin?

- Histones help in packaging DNA into a compact structure and regulate gene expression.

69. Glossary

- ❖ **Agarose Gel Electrophoresis:** A technique used to separate nucleic acids based on size by applying an electric field.
- ❖ **Aseptic Technique:** Procedures used to prevent contamination of samples by microorganisms.
- ❖ **Biochemical Tests:** Tests performed to identify bacteria based on their metabolic activities.
- ❖ **Callus:** An undifferentiated mass of plant cells grown in culture.
- ❖ **Chromatography:** A technique for separating components of a mixture based on their physical properties.
- ❖ **Cytosol:** The liquid component of the cytoplasm in which organelles are suspended.
- ❖ **Denaturation:** A process where proteins or nucleic acids lose their structure due to external stress.
- ❖ **Electrophoresis:** A method used to separate macromolecules based on charge and size.
- ❖ **Enzyme-Linked Immunosorbent Assay (ELISA):** A test used to detect and measure antibodies or antigens in a sample.
- ❖ **Fluorescence Microscopy:** A technique to visualize structures using fluorescent dyes.
- ❖ **Genetic Transformation:** The introduction of foreign DNA into an organism to change its characteristics.
- ❖ **Hemocytometer:** A device used for counting cells in a known volume of liquid.
- ❖ **Hybridization:** The process of combining complementary DNA or RNA strands.
- ❖ **Immunoprecipitation:** A method used to isolate a specific antigen from a mixture using an antibody.
- ❖ **Microbial Culture:** The growth of microorganisms in controlled laboratory conditions.

- ❖ **Plasmid:** A small, circular piece of DNA that can replicate independently within a bacterial cell.
- ❖ **Polymerase Chain Reaction (PCR):** A method used to amplify DNA sequences.
- ❖ **Spectrophotometer:** An instrument used to measure the absorbance of light by a sample at a specific wavelength.
- ❖ **Sterilization:** The process of eliminating all forms of microbial life.
- ❖ **Transformation:** The process of introducing foreign DNA into a cell.
- ❖ **Western Blotting:** A technique used to detect specific proteins in a sample using antibodies.
- ❖ **Zymogram:** A technique used to detect enzyme activity in a gel electrophoresis setting.

70. List of Instruments and Their Working Principles

1. **Spectrophotometer:** Measures the absorbance of light by a sample at a specific wavelength to determine concentration.

2. **pH Meter:** Measures the acidity or alkalinity of a solution by detecting hydrogen ion activity.

3. **Centrifuge:** Separates components of a mixture based on their density by spinning at high speeds.

4. **Laminar Air Flow Hood (LAF):** Provides a sterile working environment by directing filtered air in a uniform flow.

   Types of LAF Hoods: Horizontal LAF Hood: Air flows parallel to the work surface, providing protection to the sample. **Vertical LAF Hood:** Air flows downward onto the work surface, offering protection to both the user and sample.

5. **Autoclave:** Uses steam under pressure to sterilize laboratory equipment and media.

6. **Electrophoresis Apparatus:** Separates nucleic acids or proteins based on their size and charge under an electric field.

7. **PCR Machine (Thermocycler):** Amplifies DNA sequences by cycling through specific temperature conditions.

8. **Microscope (Compound and Phase Contrast):** Magnifies small objects for visualization of cellular structures.

9. **Colony Counter:** Counts bacterial colonies on agar plates for quantitative analysis.

10. **Microtome:** Cuts thin sections of specimens for microscopic examination.

11. **Incubator:** Provides a controlled environment for the growth of microbial and cell cultures.

12. **HPLC (High-Performance Liquid Chromatography):** Separates, identifies, and quantifies components in a mixture.

13. **Gas Chromatograph:** Analyzes volatile compounds by separating them based on their retention times.

14. **Sonicator:** Uses ultrasonic waves to disrupt cells or homogenize samples.

15. **Hemocytometer:** A counting chamber used to estimate cell concentration in a given volume.

16. **Biosafety Cabinet:** Protects the user and the environment from exposure to biohazards during microbiological work.

17. **Fume Hood:** Provides ventilation to remove hazardous chemical fumes during experiments.

18. **ELISA Reader:** Measures absorbance of samples in enzyme-linked immunosorbent assays.

19. **Lyophilizer (Freeze Dryer):** Removes water from samples through sublimation under low pressure.

20. **Fluorometer:** Measures fluorescence emitted by specific compounds to analyze molecular interactions.

21. **Western Blot Apparatus:** Used to separate and detect proteins based on size and antibody specificity.

22. **NanoDrop Spectrophotometer:** Measures nucleic acid and protein concentrations with minimal sample volume.

23. **Orbital Shaker:** Provides consistent shaking for cell culture and chemical reactions.

24. **Flow Cytometer:** Analyzes and sorts cells based on their physical and fluorescent properties.

25. **Cryostat:** Used for sectioning frozen tissue samples for microscopic analysis.

www.ingramcontent.com/pod-product-compliance
Lightning Source LLC
Chambersburg PA
CBHW040740120726